THE *ASEAN* STATES AND REGIONAL SECURITY

THE *ASEAN* STATES
AND REGIONAL SECURITY

SHELDON W. SIMON

HOOVER INSTITUTION PRESS
Stanford University, Stanford, California

The maps appearing in this book are reprinted with permission:
Map 1, Map 3: Reviewmap by Frank Tam. Courtesy of *Far Eastern Economic Review*.
Map 2: Courtesy of *Vietnam Today*.
Map 4: © by the New York Times Company. Reprinted by permission.
Map 5: Courtesy of *Far Eastern Economic Review*.

Hoover Press Publication 267

© 1982 by the Board of Trustees of the
Leland Stanford Junior University

All rights reserved
International Standard Book Number: 0-8179-7672-8
Library of Congress Catalog Card Number: 81-83852
Printed in the United States of America

.

88 87 86 85 84   9 8 7 6 5 4 3 2

To the memory of my father
Blair Simon

CONTENTS

TABLES AND MAPS

Tables

Maps

EDITOR'S FOREWORD

In the 1970s the Asian-Pacific basin countries ranked among the most rapidly developing regions of the world. Many of them began to have a larger volume of trade with the United States than do some of its West European allies. Certain ASEAN members had even begun to develop high-technology industries and seek more American financing as well as expertise. This progress occurred even though U.S. influence in the region steadily declined, a process speeded up in the mid-1970s by the American military withdrawal from Southeast Asia.

A new community of nations is taking shape among the Asian-Pacific basin states. It will play a significant role in security affairs and international politics throughout the region. ASEAN comprises five modernizing countries with many similarities and common problems. The Philippines, Indonesia, Malaysia, Singapore, and Thailand are all multi-ethnic societies with diverse cultures and languages. The five experienced rapid economic growth during the 1970s and are expected to repeat this performance during the 1980s. Malaysia and Indonesia have done better in the area of increasing food and industrial crop supplies, but all five have great potential for rapid export growth and gradual employment expansion.

The five ASEAN members share similar domestic political problems and are ruled by powerful leaders. They receive support from political factions made up of influential business groups, the military, and urban elites. All are now and will continue in the future to experience social stresses arising from rapid modernization. The ability to provide for peaceful domestic changes to cope with these stresses is crucial to the long-term prospects for success of the ASEAN five. A major factor governing this outcome, however, will be the ability of these five members to cooperate and work out a foreign policy that deals with the conflicts presently simmering in Indochina.

These conflicts and the complex involvement of various foreign powers like China and the Soviet Union continue to threaten the peace and security of Southeast Asia. The war in Cambodia (Kampuchea) provides the opportunity for greater Soviet intervention in the region.

It is to the credit of ASEAN leaders that they have held frequent consultations and worked out mutually satisfactory arrangements for containing that conflict, dealing with the serious problems it has created (for example, refugees from Vietnam), and blocking expansion of Soviet influence. How the organization has survived and continued to flourish is the subject of this timely study by Professor Sheldon W. Simon of Arizona State University. A frequent visitor to the ASEAN countries, he also has studied the literature written about the region during the past fifteen years.

This balanced and insightful analysis of how ASEAN leaders perceive their current security problems and the various possibilities open to them should interest policymakers and students of Asian international affairs. In taking the organization's activities up to the present, the author gives us a lucid account of Southeast Asia's prospects for peace and/or conflict in the 1980s. This issue will continue to influence American security interests in the Pacific. It is one that our leaders cannot afford to ignore.

RICHARD F. STAAR

Director, International Studies Program
Hoover Institution

PREFACE

The Association of Southeast Asian Nations (ASEAN) was formed in 1967 during a time of political transition in the region. The last vestiges of colonialism had disappeared; yet great-power conflict persisted through the Indochina war and the Sino-Soviet and Sino-American confrontations. Although all five ASEAN members—Malaysia, Indonesia, the Philippines, Thailand, and Singapore—were politically pro-Western and had private enterprise economies, they foresaw the possibility of an American military exit from Southeast Asia regardless of the outcome of the war in Vietnam. Great Britain's 1965 decision to withdraw its forces from Malaysia and Singapore seemed to portend a time when external mentors would no longer be available to provide security assistance against local communist adversaries and their Soviet and Chinese backers.

The time was ripe in the late 1960s, then, to devise a new form of regional association for noncommunist Southeast Asian states—more self-reliant, committed to protecting their integrity and promoting mutual economic development through policy consultations. Thus, ASEAN was conceived as a multipurpose organization whose ostensible activities were social and economic cooperation but whose underlying raison d'etre lay in political coordination to cope with a still threatening regional environment.

For the Association's first decade, economic cooperation was stymied by difficulties involved in reconciling competitive raw material–based, labor-intensive economies. There was little interest in adopting a regional perspective for growth or in coordinating industrial plans, but the events of 1975, specifically the American defeat in Vietnam, served as a catalyst for change in ASEAN. The five realized that unity was their best hope for protection against a victorious Vietnam, potentially backed by both the Soviet Union and China. Only a strong, stable ASEAN could show outsiders that its members were not the proverbial row of dominoes.

The purpose of this study is to explore the process by which the ASEAN states developed these security interests and policies, to assess the Association's relations with major external actors, and to project alternative possibilities for Southeast Asia's future and ASEAN's role within it. If the future of global politics is best understood in terms of regional clusters, ASEAN is a most important institution for study. On its success depends the future of pluralist societies in one of the most rapidly industrializing and strategically located regions of the world.

This study of ASEAN's growing role in Asian security affairs could not have been written without the assistance of a number of individuals who gave generously of their expertise and time through numerous interviews in this country and throughout Asia. They included government officials, military officers, university specialists on Asian security matters, and representatives of the research community. Where permitted, I have acknowledged their assistance by name, but in most instances where officials were interviewed, anonymity was a condition. I express my gratitude to them all.

Financial support for research in East Asia during the summers of 1979 and 1981 as well as research grants for the time required to compose this study came from a variety of institutions, including the Earhart Foundation of Ann Arbor, Michigan; the U.S. International Communication Agency, which also assisted in arranging interviews in Asia; the Hoover Institution summer grant program; the Arizona State University Liberal Arts Dean's research fund, and the new Phoenix-based Pacific Basin Institute. Without their generous aid, the time and travel necessary to complete this study would not have been possible.

Particular appreciation is due Franklin Weinstein, director of the Asian Security Studies Project at Stanford University, for his careful and thoughtful comments on an earlier draft of this study.

Special thanks are extended to Paula Martinez and Betty Parker, who labored through the author's handwritten manuscript to prepare a typed draft. And finally, at the top of my list of those to whom gratitude should be extended for their gracious willingness to share husband and father with his muse, deep appreciation goes to my wife, Charlann, and son, Alex.

1 | SECURITY CONCERNS IN SOUTHEAST ASIA

Optimists welcomed the end of the second Indochina war in 1975 as a harbinger of peace for Southeast Asia. The last major Western effort to order regional politics had failed, and America's subsequent military withdrawal from the mainland would permit the states of the region to develop their own modus vivendi, unimpeded by outsiders for the first time in over a century. Less euphoric observers pointed out that Washington's Indochina defeat did not remove the region from global politics but left it rather to the tender mercies of the victors—the Socialist Republic of Vietnam (SRV), China, and the Soviet Union. Pressure from these states would inevitably transform Southeast Asia into an appendage of the socialist camp, curtailing its political ties with the West and shifting its economic orientation to the member-states of the Council for Mutual Economic Assistance (COMECON) and/or China and Vietnam.

By the early 1980s, neither of these scenarios had come to pass. Two features of the current environment in particular had been overlooked: internecine strife among the communist actors in Southeast Asia and the ability of the noncommunist, private enterprise and foreign investment-oriented states to cooperate in the promotion of their political security and economic growth. This study examines these regional characteristics in some detail. It is particularly concerned with the manner in which Southeast Asia's newest and most important political organization, ASEAN (Association of Southeast Asian Nations, comprising

Indonesia, Malaysia, Singapore, Thailand, and Philippines) has coped with security challenges and opportunities. The former emanate from Vietnam, the USSR, and to a smaller degree China, while the latter are inherent in the Association members' own halting efforts to carve out an autonomous sphere of political security with the assistance of the United States, other Western powers, and Japan. The challenge in this context lies in establishing pacific relations with contentious communist neighbors (the PRC and Indochina) while convincing the United States to retain a military presence in the region without becoming incorporated once again into Washington's network. Put another way, the ASEAN states strive to insure their individual and collective integrity, preferably through the establishment of cordial ties with their communist neighbors. In the absence of such assurances of secure borders, however, they seem increasingly willing to engage in bilateral and multilateral efforts to protect their territories and even reluctantly to call upon outside powers—particularly the United States—to assist in these efforts in the event of direct military confrontations. The tension inherent in these two approaches results from Vietnamese and Soviet perceptions that continued reliance on the United States means that the ASEAN countries remain a part of the American security system and hence adversaries. In the resulting political vicious circle, the ASEAN states urge a continued American military commitment because of perceived Vietnamese and Soviet hostility, while the latter insist that cordial relations with ASEAN members can develop only if they abandon what remains of the American security umbrella. ASEAN diplomacy is the attempt to reconcile these conflicting pressures.

The outside guarantees used by the ASEAN states are remnants of the era of Anglo-American ascendancy—a small British and Australian air force contingent in Malaysia and bilateral security agreements between the United States and the Philippines (a treaty) and the United States and Thailand (an executive agreement—the 1962 Rusk-Thanat statement). These are not the kinds of pillars on which to base security policies, but their ineffectiveness need not be a cause for alarm. Most observers agree that the primary security challenges emanate from domestic instability that must be handled internally rather than from external attack deterrable through credible extraregional alliance arrangements. Indeed, the reliability of outside assistance to Third World governments in Southeast Asia may be increasingly problematic. The United States is unwilling in the aftermath of the Indochina war to provide unquestioning support to regimes experiencing domestic turmoil, particularly if that turmoil is attributable to repressive policies of an unpopular leadership. The post-Shah Iranian experience reinforced this

U.S. tendency not to associate too closely or exclusively with troubled authoritarian regimes. To do so would be to entangle America's security with countries in which coups, expropriations, revolutions, externally supported subversion, and thrusts by irredentist states are highly probable.[1] While the Reagan administration seems more willing to associate publicly with friendly authoritarian states than was its predecessor (witness Vice-President George Bush's praise for Marcos as a "great democrat" after the Philippine president formally repealed martial law in 1981), nevertheless, the United States seems no more willing to strengthen its military commitments to the survival of incumbents.

The ASEAN states understand U.S. ambivalence about military commitments to their regimes' survival. The growing belief that the benevolence of outsiders is uncertain in the event of major security challenges is responsible for the evolution of the indigenous security cooperation discussed in this study. Although regional associations composed of smaller states may not add significantly to their military capacity, they can prevent diplomatic isolation and enhance the bargaining abilities of their members with outsiders. ASEAN initiated this kind of collaboration as early as 1971 when its members agreed to exchange information on their individual dialogues with China to avoid competition in establishing new relationships with Asia's largest state. This experience demonstrated the advantages smaller states could derive from coordinating their diplomacy; it was subsequently repeated in negotiations over the recognition of Vietnam and Cambodia and more recently in direct annual meetings between ASEAN and the European Economic Community (EEC), the United States, and Japan.

ASEAN's efforts have underlined the variability of Southeast Asian security. Virtually every kind of arrangement has been or is being tried by one or more of its members, from informal understandings (border cooperation between Indonesia and Malaysia) through alliances with external guarantors (the Philippines-U.S. security treaty) to professions of nonalignment as an ultimate regional goal (ASEAN's ZOPFAN—the Zone of Peace, Freedom, and Neutrality). The absence of an overarching security umbrella, however, may well reflect an inchoate situation in which the actors hesitate to commit themselves to one another because the level of mutual trust and of articulation of common interests remains low. In these cases, informal understandings may be preferable to formal documents since they are easier to modify as events unfold.[2] Thus, Malaysia's cooperation with Indonesia and Thailand over border insurgencies could create an impetus for Malaysian-Philippine efforts to control the smuggling of arms to the Moro Liberation Front in Mindanao. That is, Kuala Lumpur's successful security collaboration with two other

ASEAN states could persuade Manila of Malaysia's benevolent intentions. Although their legal conflict over Sabah remains unsettled, the Philippines and Malaysia could still collaborate informally to control insurgent activity, thus increasing the reservoir of goodwill required to resolve the Sabah dispute.

The thrust of this argument is that intra-ASEAN conflicts need not preclude mutual security collaboration with respect to parallel insurgencies or obstruct the creation of a common front vis-à-vis outside actors. Furthermore, successful bilateral and trilateral collaboration could create the positive political foundation for amicable resolution of intra-ASEAN disputes.

Military Guarantees and Their Problems

While the ASEAN states have differed over the kind of regional order they should seek and the preferred timetable for the termination of external guarantors in the form of U.S. bases in the Philippines and the Five Power Defense Agreement for Malaysia and Singapore, they have agreed on the kind of political development they wish to discourage. The five are strongly anticommunist in their domestic politics. All face indigenous communist underground opposition, varying in strength from country to country. Four of the five have hosted Western military bases. The Association's 1970 Jakarta Conference on Cambodia was clearly an anticommunist gathering. More recently the five have vigorously and publicly opposed Vietnam's hegemonic position in Indochina, though differing privately over the degree of Vietnam's threat to the region. In sum, although ASEAN has endorsed a proposal for regional order that requires Indochina's inclusion to be effective—ZOP-FAN—the Association remains staunchly anticommunist. The consequent adversarial relationship with Hanoi renders any effective security collaboration between ASEAN and Indochina unlikely. Neither side accepts the other's professions of nonalignment. Each points to its opponent's ties to outside powers.

There is, indeed, considerable tension between the desire of some ASEAN elites for complete nonalignment as a signification of their states' autonomy and their more pragmatic realization that communist adversaries—particularly a Soviet-backed Vietnam—can be deterred only by the maintenance of Western forces in the region and formal U.S. commitments to at least some ASEAN members. ZOPFAN and the Nixon Doctrine, although each designed to achieve regional stability, approached that end from two different conceptualizations. ZOPFAN was to come into existence when outside powers agreed to disengage from Southeast Asia militarily. But the Nixon Doctrine—still the basis of U.S. policy in the region—emphasized U.S.-assisted defense buildups among the noncommunist states of the region and encouraged these states to create an indigenous regional defense arrangement.[3] Little wonder that Moscow and Hanoi saw the Nixon Doctrine and ASEAN as devices for maintaining an American security presence in Southeast Asia at a lower and politically more acceptable price for the U.S. public.

Despite the Vietnam debacle, American strategists agree on the importance of assisting the ASEAN states to maintain their autonomy and Western orientation for several reasons. (1) ASEAN is seen as part of a forward defense line against any attack across the Pacific. (2) Its position astride the waterways linking the Indian Ocean, South China Sea, and Pacific Ocean is vital to the flow of Japanese commerce. (3) The five contain a rich reservoir of raw materials and constitute a growing market for U.S. investment. And (4) the five are determined to keep the strategic Malacca, Lombok, and Makassar straits open for international trade.

Toward the end of the second Indochina war, the ASEAN states had reservations about continued reliance on the United States, given its much lower military profile. Indonesian elites in the early 1970s told Stanford political scientist Frank Weinstein that Jakarta should not affiliate with a military pact for various reasons: an alliance would impair the country's image of independence; it would " 'run the real risk of ending up like the Philippines, a country with no real identity of its own' "; pacts are irrelevant to internal subversion; they formalize an adversarial status with respect to other countries and hence limit the scope of one's foreign policy.[4] Perhaps, the most telling criticism of continued reliance on U.S. military guarantees lies in the member-states' assessment that American military intervention would most likely occur in the least probable contingency for ASEAN—direct, conventional aggression by a communist state. In contrast, the primary security problem facing most of ASEAN's members is externally backed internal subversion, a type of challenge least likely to elicit an American response.[5]

American policymakers find themselves in a dilemma. The ASEAN states solicit U.S. assistance and protection, but vilify any political conditions as great-power interference in small-state internal affairs. Small wonder that President Carter exclaimed with perplexity:

In many languages and out of many unfamiliar cultures other peoples constantly ask America for a response to myriad—and often conflicting—concerns. Nations ask us for leadership, but at the same time they demand their own independence of action. They ask us for aid, but they reject interference. They ask for understanding, yet they often decline to understand us in return. Some ask for protection but are wary of the obligations of alliance. Others ask for firmness and certainty, but at the same time they demand flexibility required by the pace of change and the subtlety of events. The world asks, with impatience, for all these things at once. They ask for them today, not tomorrow.[6]

Washington appears to have halted, if not yet reversed, the reduction of American forces in East Asia after the Soviet-supported Vietnamese occupation of Cambodia and Laos in early 1979. Prior to these events, U.S. forces attached to the Pacific Command had fallen to their lowest level since the end of World War II. Military aid was withheld in an attempt to change the human rights practices of allies such as the Philippines. Indeed, military assistance to Southeast Asia declined generally between 1975 and 1979 as the U.S. Congress reflected the public's belief that America must not become involved in this region's internal security problems again.

Illustrative of the disillusion with military guarantees during this period were the protracted negotiations between Washington and Manila over the renewal of the U.S. base agreements. The Philippines was concerned about the credibility of the American defense commitment, particularly since the Marcos government was contesting ownership of the potentially oil-rich Spratly Islands with China and Vietnam. Marcos wanted an explicit American endorsement of the Philippine claim and an understanding that the United States would provide military assistance in the event of conflict growing out of the dispute.[7] American legislators, however, displayed reduced interest in the Philippine bases. No longer was there a U.S. treaty commitment to Thailand. Therefore, critics argued, why not move U.S. air power back to Guam? Broader strategic concerns did not enter the debate at this time. Little was said about the importance of maintaining U.S. air forces at Clark Airbase in the Philippines to signify the continued willingness of the United States to deter Soviet and Vietnamese aggression against the ASEAN states, especially given the various conflicts of national jurisdiction over island chains in the South China Sea. To argue along these lines in the late 1970s would reactivate the Vietnam war syndrome among a substantial number of American congressmen.

Instead of sustaining previous levels of military assistance to the region, Congress cut military aid to the Philippines by 15 percent in 1977 as a pointed expression of its displeasure over human rights violations in that country. Congressional debate focused less on the strategic reasoning behind a forward American East Asian presence and more on the propriety of U.S. involvement with regimes that mistreat their own people, even if these regimes were allied with the United States.[8]

At a conference in Bali in June 1977, ASEAN notables deplored America's apparent disregard of the region. They feared that in the course of Washington's exploration of new ties with Vietnam and China, the ASEAN states' needs had been virtually ignored and that the human rights focus in the Carter administration was primarily an excuse to disengage from aid commitments to the region. Malaysia's home minister, Ghazali Shafie, explained that ASEAN did not expect the resurrection of the Southeast Asian Treaty Organization (SEATO) but rather a long-term American commitment to remain involved in the region through naval and air forces and the kind of continuous assistance necessary to develop their economies in order to sustain independence.[9] The general debate at the time within the U.S. government over American global defense reinforced ASEAN fears, for it suggested that the United States was putting its resources almost exclusively into the NATO theater and decreasing support for the U.S. Navy—the most important service for Asian requirements.[10]

American officials attempted to correct this impression of disinterest. In a major policy address in early 1978, Secretary of Defense Harold Brown recounted the major forces in the western Pacific, including B-52s, ballistic missile submarines, nine U.S. tactical fighter squadrons, two aircraft carriers, two amphibious ready groups, twenty cruisers and destroyers, two-thirds of a marine division, and a marine air wing. In short, the United States did in fact have forces on station sufficient to deter aggression against the ASEAN states and maintain freedom of the seas. Moreover, Brown asserted, by 1983, U.S. forces in the western Pacific would be strengthened through the introduction of several advanced weapons systems, including Trident missiles for the submarine fleet, cruise missiles for the B-52s on Guam, F-14 fighters for the carriers, F-15s for the air force, and AWACS (aerial warning and control systems) for all of them.[11]

This Asian reorientation was underscored after the Vietnam-Cambodian and Sino-Vietnam hostilities of early 1979. Carter administration officials foresaw a new period of tension in Southeast Asian politics in which the previous conflict between communist and pro-Western forces would be replaced by a new era of protracted competition between China and the Soviet Union for influence in the region. To help the noncommunist states maintain their autonomy under these new conditions, the United States offered increased military and economic assistance to Thailand as well as to the other ASEAN states if requested.

The ASEAN states' perception of a more aggressive Sino-Soviet competition in the region also worked to keep the United States involved. Whereas under the Nixon administration, the Philippines had insisted on $1 billion to renew the bases agreement and a U.S. commitment to back Philippine claims to the Spratlys and to provide assistance against the Moro Rebellion, the actual treaty (concluded on the last day of 1978) gave the Philippines only half that dollar amount in aid—not rent—and included no new U.S. commitments to Philippine security. Observers saw pressure from Manila's ASEAN partners as a major reason for Marcos's willingness to accept a much less favorable U.S. offer than the one he had turned down in 1976. Uncertainty over the future of the bases was thus resolved during a time of growing regional tension emanating from Vietnam, China, and the USSR.[12]

American diplomatic activity on Thailand's behalf in the wake of Vietnam's invasion of Cambodia drew praise from ASEAN media.[13] The Carter administration warned both Vietnam and the Soviet Union against any threat to Thai border areas resulting from the fighting in western Cambodia. American officials claimed that they had received assurances that Thailand's sovereignty would be respected. The United States also agreed to an additional $30 million in military aid to Thailand during Prime Minister Kriangsak Chamanan's 1979 visit to Washington, a symbol of the continued U.S. commitment to that country's integrity. The Reagan administration raised the foreign military sales credit to Thailand to $80 million for fiscal 1982.[14]

The United States was not the only power assisting ASEAN in the face of Vietnamese belligerency. China, too, appeared interested in playing the role of guarantor in Southeast Asia. In the context of its competition with Vietnam and the USSR, Vice-Premier Deng Xiaoping pledged the PRC's assistance should Thai security be threatened; he also promised unspecified support to the Philippines.[15]

The desire for outside guarantees to cope with new communist challenges was mixed with considerable ambivalence, however, given ASEAN's continued suspicion over the credibility of U.S. commitments, its mistrust of China, and the underlying belief that its security could best be insured through continued indigenous efforts aimed at neutralizing the region. Thus, Indonesia's foriegn minister, Mochtar Kusumaatmadja, saw no need for any increase in America's military forces in Southeast Asia and urged that Washington exert diplomatic influence on both China and the USSR to reduce the level of tension.[16]

Mochtar may well have been indirectly expressing Indonesia's concern over a possible Sino-American entente, which, over the long run, would enhance the PRC's regional influence to Indonesia's disadvantage. Despite the Philippines' renewed support for the U.S. forces in its territory, Marcos strongly reiterated ASEAN's commitment to regional neutrality when current challenges to peace and security had atrophied.[17] Meanwhile, American military facilities should be viewed as temporary—a point of view completely consonant with Indonesia's position, which was adopted in the formative ASEAN document of 1967.

In effect, the ASEAN states appeared caught on the horns of a dilemma. A belligerent Vietnam backed by the Soviet Union confronted a China that insisted on becoming a major actor in Southeast Asia. These threats to regional autonomy precipitated a new ASEAN appeal to the United States to remain militarily involved in the region through air and naval deployments, to increase military assistance on concessionary terms to the five, and to exert its diplomatic influence in support of ASEAN efforts to force Vietnam back to its own borders. These appeals to the United States were diluted, however, by skepticism over American willingness to provide Southeast Asia with either the military wherewithal or the foreign policy priority necessary to balance the Russians and Vietnamese and by the growing fear that a repolarization of regional politics would destroy hopes for ZOPFAN in the longer term.

Regional Self-Help and Outside Guarantees

If the ASEAN states viewed outside security commitments with ambivalence, it was because they reflected the disparity between their preferred security future of nonalignment and the realities of regional politics in the late 1970s and early 1980s. Military weakness, societal fissures, and a threatening neighbor moved the five both to ask the United States to reinforce its commitments and to request that Britain, Australia, and New Zealand retain their limited air forces in Malaysia. Reliance on outsiders remained an integral component of ASEAN security planning; hence its preference for nonalignment and desire to remove the region from great-power tensions receded ever further into the future. Most disconcerting of all—especially to Indonesia—was the appearance of increasing reliance on China as a result of the Vietnamese occupation of Cambodia. Insofar as Chinese and ASEAN diplomacy took comparable paths against Vietnam, the five were drawn into the Sino-Soviet conflict—a posture they had managed to avoid through both the first and the second Indochina wars. Much of ASEAN's current diplomatic efforts to assure regional security, then, should be viewed in the context of pragmatically maintaining outside guarantees while publicly emphasizing the commitment to nonalignment and a reduction in great-power activities in Southeast Asia. The contradiction inherent in these positions is apparent.

The movement toward regional political coordination found in ASEAN activities between the late 1960s and early 1980s demonstrates a number of advantages offered when a larger unit is created in a region composed of smaller ones. First of all, the larger unit offers a greater sense of security against predatory neighbors. Second, it provides more negotiating clout through a common stand vis-à-vis third parties. Coordinated diplomacy inhibits large outside actors from benefiting from a "divide-and-conquer" strategy with the five and hence undermining their predetermined position. Predetermined bargaining stances have been particularly useful to ASEAN in its economic negotiations, beginning in 1978 with Japan, the EEC, and the United States. From the perspective of regional integration, successful cooperation over time may internalize cooperative values, creating a stronger political and psychological identity. The reverse could equally occur, however. Diplomatic failures to elicit external agreement with ASEAN positions could lead to the re-emergence of bilateral disputes among the five, which remain just below the surface of their interactions. Outsiders could exploit a revival of these internecine tensions to break ASEAN solidarity and dissipate the advantages of coordinated diplomacy. Such actions may be expected particularly from adversaries of the regional organization. Thus, in 1977, Hanoi suggested ASEAN's replacement by a larger grouping that would embrace Burma and the three Indochina states. This new organization, Hanoi argued, would downplay ideology and confine its activities to economic cooperation.[18] In short, Hanoi wanted to see a formidable regional adversary, whose activities increasingly included informal security coordination, dissolved or at least reduced to an economic debating society.

But ASEAN meant a great deal more to each of its members, although reasons for affiliation differed. For Indonesia, ASEAN provided an opportunity to legitimate its regional leadership aspirations after years of confrontation under Sukarno. For Thailand, ASEAN membership was a mechanism for redressing the imbalance in a foreign policy that had become overreliant on the United States during the second Indochina war. Membership in a regional, ostensibly nonaligned group would signify a return to Bangkok's traditionally flexible diplomacy. Similarly the Philippines could diversify its foreign alignment risks as ASEAN provided an alternative to what appeared to be a declining American interest in Southeast Asia. Moreover, loosening its ties to Washington and joining a regional organization enhanced the Philippines' credentials as an independent Asian state rather than a mere U.S. client. For Malaysia, ASEAN signified the end of its conflict with Indonesia. The least enthusiastic ASEAN member was probably Singapore—a globally oriented city-state that joined the Association because political survival dictated the necessity of a modus vivendi with its neighbors. Leaders in Singapore held that it would be better for Singapore to work out its economic problems and security preferences within a peaceful institutional framework than risk the possibility of being squeezed by its two large Malay neighbors. Moreover, membership in ASEAN demonstrated Singapore's commitment to Southeast Asia and helped lay to rest any lingering suspicion that the city was a Trojan horse for China.

Given the diverse situations of the ASEAN five, it is not surprising that progress toward security coordination has been slow and essentially a reaction to external developments. The first significant agreement was the 1971 Kuala Lumpur Declaration, which called for the creation of a ZOPFAN in Southeast Asia. Its realization, however, was premised on two conditions, neither of which has been established: the successful removal of big-power hegemonial competition from the region; and the development of an arrangement tying the Indochinese states to ASEAN so that confrontation would be avoided. Moreover, at least three ASEAN states—Thailand, Indonesia, and Singapore—displayed little enthusiasm for a neutral zone in which its members remained vulnerable to externally backed internal insurgencies. Both Indonesia and Thailand wanted to see the establishment of national self-reliance (or, as Indonesia put it, "resilience") and regional cooperation before attempting neutralization. Obviously, for a neutral zone to succeed, its members must first display enough internal strength to withstand both regional and outside pressures toward domination. This implied a commitment to a growing regional military capability and ultimately armed rather than unarmed neutrality.[19]

This notion of armed stability was advanced in the February 1976 Bali Summit's Declaration of ASEAN Concord and the Treaty of Amity and Cooperation in Southeast Asia. The declaration was the most overtly political document issued by ASEAN since its 1967 inception. It came out of a milieu of concern over Vietnam's intentions in the wake of communist victories in Indochina. The declaration stated that "the stability of each member state and of the ASEAN region is an essential contribution to international peace and security. Each member state resolves to eliminate threats posed by subversion to its stability, thus strengthening national and regional resilience." Touching on security, the declaration called for "continuation of cooperation on a non-ASEAN basis between the member states in security matters in accordance with their mutual needs and interests." In effect, ASEAN went on record endorsing collaborative security activities potentially all the way up to the regional level as long as they met "mutual needs and interests."

The Bali Declaration implicitly acknowledged that neutralization would not evolve through the guarantees of outside powers since at least two of those powers have no interest in supporting an arrangement designed to guarantee the status quo. The Soviet Union prefers to see Southeast Asia as a component of its incipient Asian collective security system, of which the 1979 USSR-Vietnam pact is the regional cornerstone. The SRV foresees the possibility of replacing China as the revolutionary mentor of regional insurgencies. To counter these external threats, ASEAN leaders agree that national military capabilities must be strengthened.[20]

Hanoi's performance at the 1976 Colombo Conference of Non-aligned States through its Laotian client's vicious attack on ZOPFAN served to underscore the fears expressed in the Bali Declaration. The Indochinese argued in Colombo that no Southeast Asian state was truly nonaligned until it abrogated all security ties with "imperialist powers." The 1977 SRV-Laotian treaty also committed the Hanoi-led entente to support national liberation movements throughout the world. Although this may have been a rhetorical flourish to embarrass the PRC, which had begun to follow a more conservative foreign policy, it had the effect of widening the political gap between ASEAN and Indochina even further. Thus, in the same year, the Thai foreign minister expressed the hope that other Association members would come to his country's aid if it were attacked from the outside. An ASEAN symposium in Jakarta on the building of "national resilience" agreed that while Malaysia, Singapore, and the Philippines would emphasize socioeconomic development, Thailand, because of its special border problems, would inevitably stress the buildup of its security capabilities.[21]

The contradiction among neutralism, military threats from strong regional adversaries, and reliance upon a friendly outside ally—the United States—continued to muddy ASEAN security considerations. While the five agree that they should do what they can to strengthen their own national political systems against domestic troubles and be ready to engage in bilateral and trilateral security cooperation, there is less agreement on the role friendly external powers should play.

Since the Vietnamese invasion of Cambodia, Singapore and Thailand have clearly preferred a major new American military commitment to Southeast Asia. The other ASEAN states are not as avid. Indonesia, particularly, has opposed dependence on Western promises and military technology for some time. In its view, military dependence on an industrial power places the less developed states in a dependent relationship for replacement parts and technology. It may also create a foreign-oriented technological elite that employs scarce foreign exchange to obtain weapons systems frequently inappropriate to the security situation. Thus, instead of assisting in the creation of national and regional resilience, dependence on outsiders keeps the less developed states in a weak political condition and draws them into superpower hostilities.[22] On more parochial grounds, Indonesia seems to oppose outside involvement in regional security because it diminishes Jakarta's leadership position.

The others may simply see outside involvement as insufficient rather than as politically objectionable. Thus, Malaysia was not reassured when the Anglo-Malaysian Defense Agreement was replaced by the Five Power Defense Agreement (1971). The Australian government distinguished between *Malaya*, which it agreed was covered by the accord, and *Malaysia* (Sarawak and Sabah), which it did not include. Moreover, the five-power arrangement was not a firm defense commitment but provided only for consultation in the event of a challenge to Malaysia's integrity. Insofar as external assistance was not dependable, Malaysia may well have broached its neutralization proposal as a device to lock its neighbors into a security framework legitimizing the status quo. Malaysia had no territorial claims against the others, but both Indonesia and the Philippines had staked claims on Malaysian territory. Regional acceptance of neutralization could be an effective check on the use of coercion to promote irredentist designs.[23]

For neutralization to be effective, Malaysian leaders also believed it was essential that heretofore "pariah states" of importance to the region also be included in the understanding. Malaysia was the first of the ASEAN states to seek a new relationship with China. Supporting the PRC's bid for membership in the United Nations in 1971, Deputy Foreign Minister Tun Ismail announced: "For our self-interest we (would) like to see the neutrality of Southeast Asia; and it will be easier to persuade China if she is in the world body . . . We cannot ask Communist China to guarantee the neutrality of Southeast Asia and at the same time say we do not approve of her."[24]

Up to the Vietnamese invasion of Cambodia, the subsequent Chinese invasion of Vietnam, and the attendant refugee problems resulting from both incursions, ASEAN appeared to be establishing a reasonable modus vivendi with its more powerful mainland neighbors. ZOPFAN had as its goal the diplomatic denial of the legitimacy of outside military activity in Southeast Asia rather than the development of any kind of new regional defense arrangement. Indeed, ZOPFAN was a political position designed to reassure China, Vietnam, and the Soviet Union that the ASEAN states did not wish to continue the adversarial relationship characteristic of the Vietnam war period. ZOPFAN, if accepted by outside powers, would insure freedom from great-power interference in the region. In effect, a policy of denial had replaced that of alliance with the West. Or put another way, rather than relying on what appeared to be a departing American military, the ASEAN states sought a position that compensated for the perceived U.S. withdrawal by equally denying access to others. ZOPFAN also served to finesse the USSR's Asian collective security proposal. By broaching their own concept of regional security, the five could preempt Soviet designs and confine Russian alliances in the region to Vietnam and its clients.

The ASEAN states also attempted to win Vietnam over soon after its Indochina victory. Malaysian and Thai officials approached Hanoi in 1975, ostensibly to ask whether the SRV would consider affiliating with ASEAN. Although the approach was not a serious effort to convince Hanoi to join ASEAN, it did serve to communicate ASEAN's desire for good relations. Thailand went even further in 1976 under Prime Minister Seni Pramoj by closing all U.S. military facilities in the country as a gesture of accommodation to Vietnam.

During the period 1975–1979, however, parallel with continued diplomatic efforts to establish good working relations with Vietnam, the ASEAN states also intensified bilateral security cooperation against insurgencies within their countries. They observed each other's operations and emulated the more successful. Thus, security operations in the Thai-Malaysian border region were based on the successful Malaysian-Indonesian endeavor in Sabah and Sarawak. Jakarta rejected Hanoi's complaint that these actions constituted a new regional military alliance on the basis that the military activities were directed against subversive elements within countries and not against foreign powers.[25]

Vietnam began to modify its objections to ZOPFAN, so adamantly stated at the 1976 Colombo Conference. Foreign Minister Nguyen Duy Trinh's visit to four ASEAN capitals in late 1977 led to an apparent reversal of the SRV's position and an endorsement of the neutral zone idea. Even the Soviets seemed to follow suit in a statement that appeared in their Bangkok embassy bulletin. The Soviet statement urged that the neutral zone be broadened to embrace all of Southeast Asia.[26] Beijing cautioned the ASEAN states that behind the Soviet Union's and Vietnam's "sudden change of attitude" lay a "disguised attempt to widen the 'Indochina Federation' and the specter of the infamous 'Asian Collective Security System.' "[27]

In retrospect, Vietnam was attempting to reassure ASEAN during the late 1970s that despite the polarization of communist polities in the region, with China backing Pol Pot's regime in Cambodia and Hanoi aligning with Moscow, ASEAN need not fear a spillover. Nevertheless, the prospect of both China and the USSR becoming militarily engaged in the region—albeit through proxies—undermined one of ZOPFAN's basic premises, that great powers would not seek hegemony.

Although Hanoi had earlier denounced the maintenance of U.S. bases in the Philippines, implying that the region could not be genuinely free until the bases were closed, by late 1978, the SRV seemed to drop its objections. Since the SRV had joined COMECON, Deputy Foreign Minister Phan Hien reasoned that just as U.S. bases did not compromise the Philippines' independence, so COMECON membership did not disbar Vietnam from participation in the nonaligned movement. Phan Hien went on to promise that as an additional measure of goodwill,[28] Vietnam would not aid communist insurgents in the ASEAN region. Although this was reassuring at the time, most of the communist movements in ASEAN had traditionally been pro-Chinese and hence unlikely to be amenable to Vietnam's attempt to reassure ASEAN, given the climate of Sino-Vietnamese hostility.

ASEAN greeted the Soviet and Vietnamese endorsement of ZOP-FAN and the call for a broader Southeast Asian grouping with some apprehension. A broader association embracing Indochina and backed by the USSR would come dangerously close to Moscow's Asian collective security arrangement and could appear to align ASEAN with the USSR against China. To avoid this trap, officials from the five began to coordinate their positions prior to bilateral discussions with SRV Premier Pham Van Dong in September 1978. In the joint statements issued at the end of his visits to Thailand and the Philippines, the ASEAN members insisted on reiterating their commitment to ZOPFAN, thus leaving no doubt that they were not espousing the new Vietnamese concept. Thai and Philippine leaders also rebuffed Dong's inquiry about signing bilateral friendship treaties. The ASEAN belief was that China would interpret any such move as a step toward the Soviet Asia collective security proposal.[29] Clearly against their will, the ASEAN states were being buffeted by the political winds of the Sino-Soviet dispute and the internecine strife between Vietnam and China. ASEAN's careful diplomatic coordination in 1978 would establish a useful precedent when tensions among China, Vietnam, and the USSR boiled over into warfare in early 1979.

A Malaysian commentary summed up ASEAN's position succinctly: "While we will listen to both sides, neither side can expect any support from ASEAN. ASEAN in general, and Malaysia in particular, have made it very clear that peace in this region will not be the peace imposed by a dominant power but rather a peace arrived at by mutual respect for each of the Southeast Asian nations' right to exist."[30] Vietnam's New Year invasion of Cambodia, however, directly challenged this precept. More than any other feature in ASEAN's regional environment, the Vietnamese invasion of Cambodia, following immediately upon a series of pledges to the ASEAN states that Hanoi's intentions toward the region were peaceful, forced the five into an adversarial relationship with the SRV. ASEAN's cardinal rules for Southeast Asian security had been violated. An international dispute had been settled by force (Vietnam's occupation of Cambodia), and an outside great power (the USSR) was involved as a backer. ZOPFAN seemed particularly remote at this juncture.

Hanoi attempted to mollify ASEAN. Pham Van Dong reiterated his state's pledge to respect Thailand's territorial integrity. He offered once again to discuss with ASEAN, either collectively or on a bilateral basis, the SRV's concept of a regional neutral zone—this time inserting the words "stability and security" into its description.[31] The latter addition undoubtedly was meant to serve as the rationale for the overthrow of Pol Pot's regime, which had been threatening the security of its neighbors and upsetting regional stability.

The ASEAN states, however, remained unconvinced. Fearing that Southeast Asia was moving into a second cold war—this time pitting former communist allies against each other—the five did not want to be dragged into the fray. Nevertheless they could ignore neither the presence of Vietnam's forces on the Thai border nor the new flood of Indochinese refugees washed upon their shores or overflowing Thailand's borders. A series of summit meetings among the five in February and March 1979 led to an ASEAN-sponsored U.N. resolution calling for the withdrawal of all foreign forces from Vietnam and Cambodia. While ostensibly evenhanded, ASEAN in effect endorsed China's policy in the aftermath of its limited incursion into Vietnam. Beijing had agreed to withdraw from Vietnam and urged Vietnam to do the same with respect to Cambodia. ASEAN leaders hoped that the PRC-Vietnam conflict could be settled bilaterally but knew once outside powers (read: the USSR) became involved that Vietnam's ability to remain in Cambodia could become virtually open-ended. This would protract the danger to Thailand and increase the pressure on Bangkok's ASEAN partners to move more openly in the direction of security collaboration. Even the Malaysian defense minister, in whose capital ZOPFAN was originally conceived, told the Japanese foreign minister that ASEAN must band together to "counter the direct or indirect threat from the north."[32] Malaysian Home Minister Ghazali Shafie went even further and stated that ASEAN would have to cope with a number of potential hegemonisms in the region, including Soviet-Vietnamese and Chinese.[33]

ASEAN leaders were gratified not only that the General Assembly endorsed their U.N. resolution on Cambodia overwhelmingly but that a number of important countries agreed to follow ASEAN's lead on this issue, including the United States and EEC countries. The Association's perennial hawk, Singapore's Sinnathamby Rajaratnam, then foreign minister, also warned: "The Soviets and Vietnamese have always insisted that ASEAN should only be a vehicle for economic cooperation and nothing more. But look at what they've done in Indochina. They have moved from economic to political cooperation, and now they have become a military bloc."[34] Both Singapore's Lee Kwan Yew and Philippine Foreign Minister Carlos Romulo noted that considerable rethinking had occurred in ASEAN circles as a result of the Vietnamese invasion of Cambodia, implying that an ASEAN military framework could no longer be completely ruled out.[35] Thai officials affected a more cautious stance, however, clearly desiring not to antagonize Vietnam openly. Thus, Prime Minister Kriangsak dismissed the notion of a new military pact, stating that the current bilateral mode of military cooperation was sufficient.[36] So long as China maintained military pressure on Vietnam's northern border, the Thais probably felt reasonably secure—although this tacit arrangement with Vietnam's and Russia's major adversary must have been politically uncomfortable. Meanwhile, China was involved in a major diplomatic effort to associate itself with ASEAN's position in Southeast Asia, including the introduction of a disarmament proposal at the United Nations specifically calling for the implementation of ASEAN's ZOPFAN as a U.N. policy.[37]

Renewed acrimony between Vietnam and ASEAN was revealed at a meeting in Colombo in June 1979 of the Coordinating Bureau of the Nonaligned Conference when the old 1976 conflict between Indochina and ASEAN resurfaced. Vietnam and Laos insisted that if ZOPFAN was to be discussed, then the Vietnamese term "independence" must be added to the ASEAN term "freedom." The upshot was that the neutral zone proposal was dropped from the agenda entirely.[38]

As 1980 dawned, Laos and Cambodia launched a new effort to obtain ASEAN acceptance of Vietnam's hegemonial position. Meeting in Laos, the Indochinese foreign ministers offered to conclude bilateral nonaggression pacts with the five and to meet with them in order to "exchange views" on how "to make Southeast Asia a region of peace, independence, democracy, neutrality, stability and prosperity."[39] The

ASEAN states rejected the proposal as a transparent effort to obtain legitimacy for military aggression and to split the Association's united front in its dealings with the SRV.

How, then, has ZOPFAN as a foreign policy device for ASEAN succeeded? Is it wishful thinking, or does it still have political utility in Southeast Asia's newly polarized setting?

According to Malaysian Under Secretary for Foreign Affairs Mohammed bin Hasun, ZOPFAN is more a process than a goal. It is an ASEAN diplomatic effort consisting of national resilience, regional resilience, and equidistance from the great powers. Its purpose is to create regional political autonomy by combining economically viable and politically stable states. Hasun acknowledges that ASEAN's view of nonalignment changed in the course of the 1970s. By the end of the decade, there was general agreement that the original hope of great power–guaranteed nonalignment was chimerical. Instead, a concept more akin to Singapore's idea of an outside balance of power has developed. In effect, the competing activities of the larger states insure that no one acquires a hegemonial position, thus indirectly assuring regional nonalignment. In a balance of power mode, loose military relationships are acceptable for nonaligned states, as, for example, the Manila Pact's guarantee to Thailand and the U.S. bases in the Philippines.[40]

Although ASEAN may now accept both limited military activities in the region by outside powers and certain guarantees from friendly states, it still sees ZOPFAN as a convenient concept to insulate domestic insurgencies from outside aid. In such cases, ZOPFAN is used to exclude malevolent outsiders, in contrast to the five's acceptance of those with benevolent intentions.[41] As long as there is no actual military attack on an ASEAN member, all can claim that ZOPFAN may still be realized.

ASEAN's primary concern, of course, is how to respond if Thailand is attacked. Since the Vietnamese occupation of Cambodia, all other ASEAN members have indicated at one time or another that they would come to Thailand's assistance. How and with what, however, remain open questions. The ASEAN states must rally behind a threatened member; not to do so would spell the end of the Association. The primary Indonesian and Malaysian fears appear to focus less on an SRV thrust into Thailand and more on the prospects of a second Chinese invasion of Vietnam if Thailand is attacked. This latter development would make it appear that ASEAN had linked up with China, destroying nonalignment and placing the five squarely against Vietnam and the USSR.[42] ASEAN finds this a particularly disturbing scenario since it has no control over the actions of either Hanoi or Beijing.

Economic Security

Although this study is not concerned with ASEAN's economic growth, development, distribution, or investment strategies per se, certain economic components of security should be addressed. These include the relationships between development and stability as well as the impact of foreign investment on growth and autonomy. In a state with significant regional, linguistic, and ethnic differences, the powerholders in the central cities frequently reinforce economic disparities. These in turn may lead to frustration and ultimately political instability, undermining the social order.[43]

Certain indices suggest that some ASEAN states may be susceptible to economically induced political disorder, aggravated by the maldistribution of growth benefits. In the Philippines, for example, a virtual doubling of population by the early years of the twenty-first century, rapid urbanization, and a diminished agricultural sector spell trouble on the horizon.[44] As one Australian analyst put it:

> ASEAN members are, in varying degrees, faced with severe problems arising from poverty, unemployment, ethnic conflicts, urban-rural imbalance in access to resources, regressive fiscal systems, and limited access to social services such as education. The economic cooperation being pursued by the ASEAN members may well contribute to rising GNP, but increased wealth in societies with major socio-economic inequalities and limited political participation may not in fact result in the political stability which ASEAN is intended to promote. It could just as well result in increased social dislocation and violent political opposition with all the attendant dangers of external interference by major powers.[45]

Both Indonesia and the Philippines have experienced adverse political and social side effects from their industrial development policies. Since the early 1970s, Jakarta has emphasized heavy industry, urban growth, and high-technology programs (even in rice production). While these have led to some increase in output—although most of the country's foreign exchange earnings still come from petroleum—the distribution of this new wealth remains concentrated in Java and the cities and among the bureaucracy and its favored entrepreneurs. In the Philippines, a small group, though growing in size, has broken the United States' colonial hold on the economy; production and wealth, however, are still controlled by a few, producing costly and inefficient products for a small, protected domestic market.

Although Indonesia has provided incentives for foreign investment, including tax holidays and tariff reduction, it found that domestic businesses were being starved for capital. Most of the foreign investment went into extractive industries, moreover, re-establishing the old colonial pattern of repratriation of most economic benefits to developed investor states. Clearly, Indonesia's New Economic Order was a double-edged sword—on the one hand it elicited resources unavailable domestically, but on the other it created apprehension and discontent by skewing the capital market against local industries.

Four of the ASEAN five (Singapore excepted) face internal economic growth–political stability pressures. They hope to achieve some relief by coordinating economic policies within the Association, both to enhance their mutual bargaining power with outsiders and to assist one another in the event of economic emergencies such as short-term shortages of rice or petroleum. Indeed, ASEAN plans, particularly since the 1976 Bali Summit, seem quite ambitious. Besides the earlier agreement to lower the tariff barriers to regional trade, the Association has agreed to harmonize the allocation of major new industries in the region, swap foreign exchange reserves, create inventories of strategic commodities, and stabilize export earnings through a common fund.

Plans for industrial allocation have been largely unsuccessful, however, with only Indonesia's urea project still moving ahead. Political concerns led to the decision to scrap the most economically viable project, small diesel engines in Singapore. Indonesia already had a small diesel industry and feared it would be driven out of business if Singapore entered the market. Given Indonesia's key role in ASEAN, Singapore withdrew from the field. Even under optimal regional conditions, though, it is unlikely that industrial complementarity will be an important contributor to growth because ASEAN trade is increasingly global rather than regional (see Table 1).[46] Compared with 1971, when intraregional trade was 16.4 percent of total trade, by 1975 it had declined to 14 percent. And in 1978, it fell to about 10 percent.[47] ASEAN has found that it prospers as extraregional trade increases.

In the aggregate, ASEAN indices are rather impressive. Gross national product (GNP) growth rates in the 1970s exceeded those of the previous decade—with the exception of Thailand. Total U.S. trade with the ASEAN countries followed a similar pattern, reaching $12.5 billion in 1978. (See Table 2.) Indeed, noncommunist Southeast Asia is one of the few regions where economic growth has not slowed precipitously as a result of the global energy shortage and recession. Even in manufacturing, which is still relatively weak in Indonesia, the Philippines, and Thailand, the average annual real growth rate from 1970 to 1977 ranged from a low of 6.8 percent in the Philippines to 12.3 percent in Malaysia.[48]

The ASEAN five form something of an economic continuum. Since the mid-1960s, Singapore has developed into a modern manufacturing state and a regional trade and service center. Unlike its partners, it no longer has a labor-intensive economy and has increasingly attracted high-technology investment to the island, as well as become a capital exporter itself. As a global trading center, Singapore has supported trade liberalization and opposed protectionism. At the other end of the continuum is Indonesia, which is the least developed industrially, the most protectionist, and the least willing to engage in intra-ASEAN trade liberalization. The other three members fall in the middle with open and closed sectors of their economies coexisting.

Because of Singapore's need for good political relations with its partners, it has regularly subordinated its preference for free trade and acceded to Indonesia's concern for its infant industries. Singapore is particularly careful to maintain a low profile in ASEAN's economic deliberations (in contrast to its high-profile political role as an anticommunist hawk). As an ethnic Chinese state connected to a network of Chinese business elites throughout ASEAN, Singapore is very sensitive to potential charges that it is either a stalking-horse for the PRC or a haven for the "shady" business interests of the region's most prosperous ethnic minority. To compensate, Singapore has held its peace with respect to its ASEAN partners' protectionist policies, which have led to national manufacturing interests, heavily subsidized and sheltered from competition. Any kind of economic integration for ASEAN, then, remains far down the road, at least until the countries have developed more (complementary) economic structures.

The issue eliciting the most attention in ASEAN economic policy is foreign investment, most particularly the performance of multinational corporations (MNCs) within the five. It has been argued that on the positive side of the ledger, MNCs provide a number of benefits to host countries.[49] They constitute export platforms to earn foreign exchange, they are a source of regular and reliable tax revenues, and they engage in technology transfer and the development of a local managerial capability through in-country training. Indeed, Singapore is a prime example of how a population can prosper through MNC-led development. Malaysia, too, has benefited from MNC investment. Its sound infrastructure in the form of a professional bureaucracy, a low level of corruption, a small population/land ratio, and a sizable Chinese entrepreneurial community all serve to provide a favorable environment for MNC operations.

TABLE 1

ASEAN Direction of Trade
(millions of U.S. $)

	Total	Per-centage	United States	Per-centage	Japan	Per-centage	EEC	Per-centage
				Industrial Countries				
EXPORTS								
1964	2,218.3	70.5	718.8	23.0	682.3	21.8	533.2	17.0
1971	3,847.9	58.4	1,169.6	17.7	1,570.2	23.9	817.3	13.4
1972	686.2	59.6	1,411.2	17.9	1,918.0	24.4	1,235.4	15.7
1973	8,210.6	62.1	2,258.2	17.1	3,628.5	27.5	2,097.7	15.9
1974	13,983.5	61.9	3,919.7	17.3	6,877.9	30.4	2,633.5	11.7
1975	12,724.9	61.3	4,124.0	19.9	5,609.2	27.0	2,741.2	13.2
1971–75 average	7,612.0	60.7	2,433.6	18.0	3,381.0	26.6	1,676.4	13.6
IMPORTS								
1964	2,316.1	66.2	625.4	17.9	895.5	25.6	453.6	13.0
1971	4,995.5	62.6	1,144.8	13.3	2,083.2	26.1	1,547.0	19.4
1972	5,806.8	61.5	1,448.5	15.3	2,501.1	26.1	1,624.4	17.2
1973	8,546.1	60.2	2,272.8	16.0	3,576.1	25.1	2,345.5	16.5
1974	13,110.9	57.5	3,366.1	14.5	5,516.9	24.2	3,687.8	16.2
1975	13,450.6	57.8	3,613.6	15.5	3,679.2	15.8	2,876.6	12.4
1971–75 average	8,037.7	60.0	2,078.5	14.9	3,041.8	23.5	2,089.2	16.3

SOURCES: Computed from IMF and IBRD, Direction of Trade, Annual, 1961–1963 and 1970–1974; and IMF, Direction of Trade, December 1976, January 1977, and May 1977; quoted in Far Eastern Economic Review Yearbook, 1978, p. 71.

On the other hand, in countries with corrupt bureaucracies and leaders, MNCs buy off bureaucrats in order to do business. Governments, therefore, open themselves to allegations of selling out to foreigners. Both the Thai student revolt of 1973 that toppled the Thanom-Praphat government and the Indonesian student riots in Jakarta in January 1974 were in large part reactions against what the students perceived as the inordinate role of Japanese capital.

Another source of discontent arises from the MNC preference for working with local business elites. In Southeast Asia this by and large means the Chinese and may exacerbate racial tensions and weaken indigenous (non-Chinese) businessmen.

ASEAN		Socialist Countries				
Total	Per-centage	Total	Per-centage	China	Per-centage	Grand Total
EXPORTS						
270.4	8.6	69.9	0.3	69.9	0.3	3,131.4
1,431.1	19.4	175.1	2.7	33.4	0.5	6,594.7
1,529.4	19.6	177.2	2.3	50.2	0.6	7,857.5
2,586.3	15.9	414.3	3.1	140.5	1.1	13,214.0
3,598.8	19.2	661.2	2.9	171.4	0.8	22,608.2
3,350.0	16.1	451.2	2.2	135.3	0.6	20,765.8
2,127.7	18.0	324.8	2.6	100.1	0.7	12,361.9
IMPORTS						
327.0	9.3	139.6	4.0	139.6	4.0	3,497.4
960.0	12.0	301.5	3.7	226.6	2.8	7,979.2
1,149.0	12.1	324.1	3.4	251.7	2.7	9,442.3
1,678.4	11.8	548.5	3.8	456.8	3.2	14,197.7
2,451.4	10.7	874.5	3.8	669.6	2.9	22,313.5
2,876.6	12.4	874.6	3.8	367.0	1.6	23,260.7
1,573.7	11.8	510.5	3.7	351.9	2.6	13,531.8

NOTE: Singapore does not publish trade statistics with Indonesia; Singapore-Indonesian trade figures are obtained from the Indonesian side, which is known to be seriously downward-biased owing to some malpractices on the part of the traders.

While the ASEAN states continue to solicit foreign investment, some policy analysts in the region are having second thoughts. There is growing concern in the Philippines, for example, that the country is becoming mortgaged to foreign loans, with interest and principal repayments eating heavily into the country's development budget.[50] Complaints are also voiced about foreign domination of the modern sectors of the Philippine economy by U.S. and Japanese capital.

A separate but parallel line of argument concerns the effect of a growing protectionist stance among developed states as a result of the global recession of the late 1970s. Because the ASEAN states' exports consist primarily of semiprocessed and light industrial products, the imposition of tariff and quota barriers by developed states will decrease ASEAN's earnings precipitously. ASEAN representatives argued against increased protectionism in the developed states at the 1979 Manila United Nations Conference on Trade and Development (UNCTAD), to little avail, and expressed concern over difficulties in obtaining foreign investment for local industries that would contribute to regional self-sufficiency. Instead, Philippine officials argued, foreign business interests were too committed to short-term projects and the maintenance of host country economies in positions of dependency.[51] This approach to foreign investment was politically myopic, they warned. Only with the regional strengthening of ASEAN economies could self-sustaining growth based on both domestic and foreign markets occur. This growth, in turn, would benefit poorer segments of the population, whose stake in the politics of their respective countries is essential if the fires of insurgencies are to cool. The greater the incidence of internal insurgency, moreover, the greater the probability of outside powers attempting to cause trouble and subsequently the greater the pressure on the United States

TABLE 2

ASEAN AVERAGE GROWTH RATES

	1960–1969	1970–1977
Philippines	5.1	6.3
Indonesia	3.5	8.3
Singapore	8.8	8.9
Malaysia	6.5	7.8
Thailand	8.2	6.5

U.S.-ASEAN TRADE
(billions of U.S. dollars)

1970		2.3
1971		2.4
1972		2.9
1973		4.4
1974		7.6
1975		7.9
1976		9.5
1977		11.0
1978		12.5

SOURCE: U.S. Congress, House of Representatives, Committee on Foreign Affairs, *Security and Stability in Asia in 1979* (Washington, D.C.: Government Printing Office, 1979), p. 15.

NOTE: Trade totals differ from those given in Table 1 due to variation in sources.

to honor its commitments under the Manila Pact, mutual security treaties, and other less formal understandings between Washington and ASEAN members. In short, unless Western and Japanese businessmen adopt a more farsighted approach to investment decisions, their governments may ultimately be called upon to pay a higher political and military price to protect Third World regimes against communist-aided domestic insurgencies that feed on underdevelopment and maldistribution of the national product.

Philippine sensitivity to these concerns is certainly warranted. Although the Philippines experienced aggregate growth during the martial law period (1972–1981) of about 5 to 6 percent a year, other indices were disturbing. Philippine government figures showed a decline in real wages of workers in Manila of about 25 percent between 1973 and 1978; meanwhile the gap between the rich and poor widened into one of Asia's largest. The top 20 percent of the country's income earners accounted for 53 percent of total national income in 1977, while the bottom 40 percent took in only 14.7 percent.[52] Moreover, the nutritional level appears not to have improved since 1963. The Asian Development Bank ranks the country's per capita daily caloric intake as the lowest in Asia—below those of Indonesia, India, and even Bangladesh.[53]

Critics of President Marcos's export-led growth policy complain that by creating large foreign-owned (primarily Japanese) agrobusinesses in pineapples, copra, and bananas, the regime has driven small farmers off the land without finding alternative employment for them.[54] Migration of these people from subsistence farming areas or small market towns to regional cities has led to runaway growth of shantytown barrios, urban unemployment, malnutrition, and ultimately political turmoil. The unrest of the poor is exacerbated and may be organized and led by growing middle-class nationalist discontent, which deplores the economy's increased dependence on foreign capital.

While the communist New People's Army (NPA) is the only organized military opposition whose goal is the overthrow of the Philippine government, its numbers are small (somewhat over 7,000). Rural sympathizers may be increasing, however, as the NPA encourages mutual aid and resistance among farmers against absentee landlords. NPA successes would be a good index of organized political response to instability in the rural areas created by displaced farmers and alienated city dwellers.

Thailand is another ASEAN country with significant insurgencies that could be exacerbated by economic malaise. Its economic growth record is mixed. A 1978 World Bank report found that while the Thai economy had grown overall since the 1960s, important sectors had not.

Rain-dependent subsistence rice farmers in the north and northeast and to a less extent those in the south saw their incomes stagnate over a fifteen-year period. Interestingly, these regions also form the locus for major communist insurgencies as well as periodic ethnic minority unrest. In contrast, in the central plains, more than half the farm households abandoned rice farming for cash crops, taking advantage of the irrigation, transportation, and marketing infrastructure in the provinces around Bangkok. As a result the income of about 2.5 million farmers— 10 percent of the country's total—has doubled since 1960, though in the process many became tenants on land purchased by urban investors.[55]

A rough profile of poverty in Thailand would show about eleven million people below the poverty line, employing U.N. criteria, with eight million of those located in the rural north and northeast. Reports on both Thailand and Malaysia in 1979 found a decline in the overall number of poverty-stricken but an increase in the number of people in that category flocking to the cities.[56]

Although ASEAN has been able to do little to assist its members to overcome domestic economic strains that could lead to political instability, it has been more successful in dealing with other economic actors in the international system to enhance the Association's overall bargaining power and reduce its vulnerability. Donald Crone of the University of British Columbia has examined ASEAN trade and investment relationships with the rest of the world to see if, over time, the Association has diversified its partners and hence reduced its vulnerability (see Tables 3–9).[57] His findings on trade relationships reveal that while ASEAN's overall trade is being dispersed among a larger number of states, the specific role played by Japan has grown enormously. Nevertheless, Crone argues, ASEAN's growing trade with Japan need not place the Association at a disadvantage. Since Association members took 10.5 percent of Japan's trade in 1978, their importance to Tokyo has also increased. This means that Japan will probably be more politically responsive to ASEAN. Indeed, recent developments such as the annual Japan-ASEAN consultations and Prime Minister Fukuda Takeo's promise of $1 billion in assistance for ASEAN industrial projects represent a growing Japanese desire to develop good working relationships with the capitalist economies of the region.

Individually the five countries have experienced differing degrees of success at trade dispersion. The most successful is Singapore, which has achieved a virtually even balance among its industrial partners, thus obtaining substantial insurance against vulnerability. The Philippines has managed to reduce its overdependence on the United States as well as on Japan, but it has been less successful in luring European trade. Most

TABLE 3

ASEAN: DIRECTION OF TRADE
(percentage)

	1967	1969	1971	1973	1975	1977
Large Industrial	68.7	71.1	58.4	58.6	57.6	56.4
United States	20.3	20.8	15.9	16.4	17.6	17.7
EEC	22.2	21.1	17.4	16.1	14.6	14.5
Japan	26.2	29.2	25.1	26.1	25.4	24.2
Small Industrial	15.3	16.2	11.8	12.2	12.2	12.4
Canada	0.9	1.2	1.1	0.7	0.8	0.8
Other Western European	2.6	3.0	2.0	2.2	2.1	2.0
Australia	4.7	5.0	4.0	3.8	4.0	3.5
Newly Industrializing Countries	7.1	7.0	4.7	5.4	5.3	6.1
Third World	8.3	6.5	9.0	8.4	14.0	14.5
Latin America	1.1	1.2	1.0	1.0	2.1	1.9
West Asia	3.2	2.7	4.2	4.0	8.5	8.9
Africa	0.4	0.7	1.4	1.5	1.2	1.3
South Asia	3.6	1.9	2.4	1.9	2.2	2.4
Socialist	1.1	0.7	4.5	4.5	3.4	3.1
USSR, Eastern Europe	0.2	0.1	1.4	1.4	1.2	1.1
China	0	0	1.8	2.2	1.9	1.8
Indochina	0.9	0.6	1.3	0.9	0.3	0.1
ASEAN	6.3	5.3	15.3	14.2	12.7	13.5
*Index of Dispersion	47.67	43.08	38.68	38.61	38.30	37.95

*The smaller the number, the greater the dispersion (or the less concentrated is the trade).

TABLE 4

ASEAN: ASYMMETRY OF TRADE WITH LARGE INDUSTRIAL NATIONS

	1967	1972	1978
Trade with each, as percentage of ASEAN trade			
United States	20.3	16.6	17.7
EEC	22.2	16.6	14.3
Japan	26.2	25.6	24.9
ASEAN trade, as percentage of each country's trade			
United States	2.8	2.7	4.0
EEC	1.2	0.8	1.1
Japan	8.4	8.8	10.5

TABLE 5

SINGAPORE: DIRECTION OF TRADE
(percentage)

	1967	1969	1971	1973	1975	1977
Large Industrial	49.9	59.0	42.2	45.2	41.8	40.0
United States	8.5	13.2	12.4	15.9	15.0	13.9
EEC	21.2	21.7	15.0	15.3	13.2	12.1
Japan	20.2	24.1	14.8	14.0	13.6	14.0
Small Industrial	24.8	23.3	14.0	14.7	15.8	16.4
Third World	18.7	12.5	19.9	18.4	24.5	25.0
Socialist	3.4	1.6	8.3	6.8	4.1	3.1
ASEAN	6.9	5.0	22.0	20.0	17.1	17.4
Index of Dispersion	36.1	38.6	35.2	35.2	34.9	34.7

TABLE 6

PHILIPPINES: DIRECTION OF TRADE
(percentage)

	1967	1969	1971	1973	1975	1977
Large Industrial	81.9	79.2	78.8	78.8	70.1	65.9
United States	37.9	33.6	32.0	32.5	24.8	26.9
EEC	13.6	14.3	14.9	12.5	14.1	14.7
Japan	30.4	31.3	31.9	33.8	31.2	24.3
Small Industrial	8.5	10.6	11.5	11.4	10.5	11.7
Third World	5.5	5.0	5.2	7.5	15.0	14.9
Socialist	0.3	0.1	0.2	1.3	1.5	4.6
ASEAN	4.2	4.6	4.2	2.1	4.0	5.3
Index of Dispersion	51.0	48.8	48.4	49.3	44.4	41.5

of the slack has been taken up by trade with the Third World. Malaysia has become more vulnerable to Japan as European trade declined after 1975, while Thailand has reduced its vulnerability to Japan and degree of sensitivity to large industrial nations, shifting more of its trade to the Third World. Finally, Indonesia, more than any other ASEAN state, has become heavily dependent on Japan, with a precipitous decline in European trade as well as trade with smaller industrial nations. Indonesia remains the least diversified of the ASEAN five and very sensitive to any changes in Japanese trade. Interestingly, ASEAN's overall dependence on Japan is a result of Indonesia's situation since it accounts for 25 percent of ASEAN trade. The other four have managed to diversify

TABLE 7

MALAYSIA: DIRECTION OF TRADE
(percentage)

	1967	1969	1971	1973	1975	1977
Large Industrial	64.2	68.6	50.1	50.0	52.5	56.2
United States	13.9	18.0	9.9	9.5	13.5	15.7
EEC	27.9	24.9	21.3	21.0	21.9	18.8
Japan	22.4	25.7	18.9	19.5	17.1	21.7
Small Industrial	17.3	19.9	13.6	13.9	13.5	12.6
Third World	13.5	7.3	12.7	10.3	11.7	11.9
Socialist	0.3	0.1	5.4	7.0	5.1	4.5
ASEAN	4.9	4.2	20.9	19.9	19.9	17.1
Index of Dispersion	40.7	41.8	38.1	37.6	38.1	38.2

TABLE 8

INDONESIA: DIRECTION OF TRADE
(percentage)

	1967	1969	1971	1973	1975	1977
Large Industrial	72.5	78.4	72.6	72.2	71.1	70.6
United States	18.2	22.3	15.7	16.5	21.4	22.2
EEC	29.7	22.7	17.5	13.5	10.9	13.0
Japan	24.6	33.4	39.4	42.2	38.8	35.4
Small Industrial	19.7	14.8	3.7	5.6	8.1	8.3
Third World	2.3	1.5	4.0	5.0	9.5	8.5
Socialist	0.2	0.2	2.6	1.5	3.2	1.4
ASEAN	5.6	4.5	13.0	10.4	9.7	12.0
Index of Dispersion	44.8	47.2	48.1	49.0	47.3	46.0

among the major industrial nations. Moreover, Malaysia and Thailand are approaching the point where only half of their trade is with the major nations, and Singapore has managed to reduce its dependence on the major nations to one-third.

In a separate paper examining ASEAN's vulnerability to foreign investment concentration, Crone found that foreign companies controlled over 45 percent of total manufacturing investment in the Association. His data showed that foreign capital as a share of total investment was highest in Singapore and lowest in Thailand. (See Tables 10–15.)[58] The share of manufacturing in total GNP is increasing throughout the re-

TABLE 9

THAILAND: DIRECTION OF TRADE
(percentage)

	1967	1969	1971	1973	1975	1977
Large Industrial	66.6	68.5	66.1	62.3	60.7	55.9
United States	15.6	15.1	13.8	11.9	13.3	11.3
EEC	20.6	22.2	19.8	18.7	16.9	17.7
Japan	30.4	31.2	32.5	31.7	30.5	26.9
Small Industrial	12.3	13.8	13.2	15.5	12.3	12.4
Third World	9.7	8.4	11.1	9.0	17.5	20.2
Socialist	2.3	1.7	2.5	2.7	2.0	3.2
ASEAN	10.3	8.3	7.9	10.2	8.6	10.2
Index of Dispersion	42.3	43.1	42.2	41.6	40.7	38.4

TABLE 10

FOREIGN CAPITAL AS A SHARE OF TOTAL INVESTMENT
IN ASEAN STATES' MANUFACTURING
(percentage)

Singapore	69.4	(1975)
Philippines	59.7	(1975)
Indonesia	56.9	(1972)
Malaysia	54.8	(1976)
Thailand	29.1	(1975)

gion, as is its share in total exports, although with the exception of Singapore, that share is still relatively small.[59]

As in the realm of trade, the ASEAN states are attempting to diversify their investment sources away from undue reliance on the United States and Japan and more toward the EEC. Implementation varies from country to country. In Malaysia, for example, general foreign ownership of manufacturing is supposed to be reduced from 60 percent in 1970 to 30 percent by 1990, primarily through joint venture requirements. And, indeed, in 1977 only 2 percent of all projects approved were totally foreign owned.[60] Malaysia has utilized two techniques to dilute foreign control of the economy: insistence on joint venture capital and diversification of foreign investment sources. All of the ASEAN states see diversification as a politically expedient way of meeting nationalist concerns over economic dependence while still allowing the import of foreign investment necessary for growth. Diversification seeks to pro-

TABLE 11

INDONESIA: CUMULATIVE FOREIGN INVESTMENT
(percentage distribution)

	1967	1968	1969	1970	1971	1972	1973	1974	1975	1976
Large Industrial	91.7	60.6	57.8	58.8	55.1	58.1	58.8	62.2	69.1	67.3
United States	82.5	43.1	39.9	37.1	30.7	35.5	30.0	22.3	18.1	17.4
EEC	7.2	12.5	6.0	8.5	7.9	6.8	6.9	12.4	10.1	10.1
Japan	2.0	5.0	12.0	13.2	16.4	15.8	21.8	27.6	40.9	39.8
Small Industrial	0.8	33.2	15.0	14.7	21.4	20.7	22.8	23.2	19.0	21.1
Canada	—	18.3	6.7	5.4	4.4	3.4	2.8	2.0	1.6	1.5
Other Western Europe	—	1.3	0.7	1.8	1.4	1.2	1.2	1.8	1.5	1.4
Australasia	0.6	0.3	1.4	0.8	6.3	5.1	5.4	4.5	3.7	3.5
Newly Industrializing Countries	0.2	13.3	6.2	6.7	9.3	10.9	13.3	14.9	12.2	14.6
Third World	5.0	2.1	1.0	0.9	1.3	1.9	2.1	1.8	1.6	1.6
Latin America	5.0	2.1	1.0	0.9	1.3	1.3	1.2	0.9	0.7	0.7
Africa	—	—	—	—	—	—	.02	.01	.01	.01
South Asia	—	—	—	0.04	0.03	0.6	0.8	0.9	0.9	0.9
Socialist	—	—	—	—	—	—	—	—	0.1	.06
ASEAN	2.5	4.0	27.3	25.5	22.3	19.4	16.4	12.8	10.2	9.9
Philippines	2.5	2.2	22.6	18.6	14.9	12.0	10.2	7.6	6.0	5.8
Singapore	—	1.6	3.0	4.5	4.0	4.3	3.6	3.3	2.6	2.6
Malaysia	—	0.2	1.4	2.1	2.4	2.3	1.9	1.4	1.2	1.1
Thailand	—	—	0.3	0.3	1.0	0.7	0.6	0.5	0.4	0.3
Total	100	100	100	100	100	100	100	100	100	100
Geographical Dispersion Index	83.0	50.6	48.8	45.5	40.8	43.4	42.0	41.7	48.1	47.6
Annual Growth Rate (percentage)	—	136.8	175.1	22.8	26.2	27.5	22.1	37.3	26.5	4.8

duce competition among investors in order to reduce the inordinate influence of a few. It is, in effect, an economic balance of power doctrine, complementary to the same principle applied at the political-strategic level.

In evaluating the overall effectiveness of ASEAN's diversification in the late 1970s, Crone finds a "mixed picture."[61] In all except the Philippines, the percentage of foreign investment accounted for by the major economic powers increased, with Singapore receiving four-fifths of its investment from the major industrial nations. In contrast, however, concentration on specific major partners has been reduced so that each ASEAN country now draws from two or more major investment sources. The widespread pattern of colonial dependence prevalent through the 1960s, then, has come to an end. The geographical dispersion index demonstrates some success for all the ASEAN states with the

TABLE 12

MALAYSIA: CUMULATIVE FOREIGN INVESTMENT
(percentage distribution)

	1975	1976	1977
Large Industrial	48.7	53.2	53.2
United States	11.4	12.3	10.4
EEC	17.7	19.1	22.7
Japan	19.6	21.8	20.1
Small Industrial	19.6	17.4	16.9
Canada	1.0	1.2	0.5
Other Western Europe	2.3	2.3	1.6
Australasia	2.4	2.4	2.6
Newly Industrializing Countries	13.9	11.6	12.1
Third World	3.7	3.7	3.8
Latin America	1.7	1.6	1.7
South Asia	2.0	2.2	2.2
ASEAN	28.0	25.7	26.2
Indonesia	0.1	0.1	0.05
Philippines	0.07	0.2	0.1
Singapore	27.6	25.2	25.9
Thailand	0.2	0.2	0.1
Total	100	100	100
Geographical Dispersion Index	42.4	42.2	43.2
Annual Growth Rate (percentage)	—	23.6	32.0

TABLE 13

PHILIPPINES: CUMULATIVE FOREIGN INVESTMENT
(percentage distribution)

	1968	1969	1970	1971	1972	1973	1974	1975	1976	1977
Large Industrial	60.7	64.8	61.1	36.8	47.7	57.5	66.8	64.6	64.3	59.7
United States	59.0	60.4	55.4	32.4	40.2	41.3	30.1	29.7	30.9	29.8
EEC	0.01	2.6	3.8	1.9	3.5	9.5	10.8	10.0	9.8	8.7
Japan	1.7	1.8	1.9	2.5	4.0	6.7	25.9	24.9	23.6	21.3
Small Industrial	1.2	5.9	6.5	46.8	37.7	29.3	23.8	26.9	28.1	32.4
Canada	—	—	0.01	0.05	1.6	1.1	2.7	2.4	2.1	1.8
Other Western Europe	—	0.5	0.4	0.2	1.0	0.8	2.2	2.3	5.1	4.5
Australasia	—	—	—	—	0.02	0.1	2.2	3.5	4.3	3.8
Newly Industrializing Countries	1.2	5.4	6.1	46.6	35.1	27.2	16.7	18.7	16.7	22.4
Third World	—	—	0.3	0.2	0.2	0.6	0.8	0.9	0.8	0.7
Latin America	—	—	—	—	—	0.4	0.5	0.6	0.5	0.4
South Asia	—	—	0.3	0.2	0.2	0.2	0.3	0.3	0.3	0.3
West Asia	—	—	—	—	—	—	0.01	0.01	0.01	0.01
ASEAN	—	—	—	—	—	0.01	0.3	0.3	0.3	0.3
Indonesia	—	—	—	—	—	—	—	—	<0.01	<0.01
Singapore	—	—	—	—	—	0.01	0.2	0.2	0.2	0.2
Thailand	—	—	—	—	—	—	0.05	0.1	0.1	0.1
Not Specified	38.1	29.3	32.1	16.3	14.4	12.5	8.3	7.3	6.5	6.9
Total	100	100	100	100	100	100	100	100	100	100
Geographical Dispersion Index	61.4	62.1	57.7	57.3	54.1	51.5	44.8	44.6	44.1	44.4
Annual Growth Rate (percentage)	—	119.0	44.9	169.2	37.0	47.1	85.1	14.9	17.4	16.3

TABLE 14

SINGAPORE: CUMULATIVE FOREIGN INVESTMENT
(percentage distribution)

	1967	1968	1969	1970	1971	1972	1973	1974	1975	1976	1977	1978
Large Industrial	68.0	59.9	65.7	82.1	77.8	80.6	80.5	79.6	79.4	80.1	80.2	82.2
United States	8.9	11.7	21.8	34.5	31.8	36.8	37.3	35.4	33.1	33.0	33.0	30.5
EEC	48.8	40.7	37.8	40.8	39.1	37.8	34.3	32.6	32.8	33.1	31.9	36.4
Japan	10.2	7.5	6.0	6.8	6.9	6.0	8.9	11.6	13.4	14.0	15.3	15.3
Small Industrial	n.a.	n.a.	n.a.	n.a.	22.2	19.4	19.5	20.4	20.7	19.9	19.8	17.8
Canada					0.3	0.3	0.3	0.3	0.3	0.3	0.3	0.2
Other Western Europe					1.6	1.6	1.6	1.2	1.8	1.8	2.0	1.9
Other Asia*					20.3	17.5	17.6	18.8	18.6	17.8	17.5	15.7
Not Specified	32.0	40.1	34.3	17.9	0	0	0	0	0	0	0	0
Total	100	100	100	100	100	100	100	100	100	100	100	100
Geographical Dispersion Index	59.9	58.8	55.8	56.8	54.8	55.9	54.4	53.0	52.0	52.0	51.5	52.3
Annual Growth Rate (percentage)	—	49.8	32.2	65.8	58.3	44.9	16.5	14.9	10.7	10.6	10.9	26.5

*Includes Australasia, South Asia, Newly Industrialized Countries, and ASEAN.

TABLE 15

THAILAND: CUMULATIVE FOREIGN INVESTMENT
(percentage distribution)*

	1970	1971	1974	1975	1976	1977	1978
Large Industrial	62.4	62.9	64.3	62.6	63.2	62.6	63.0
United States	18.1	17.0	16.2	13.8	15.4	15.6	15.4
EEC	11.1	10.6	10.8	10.4	10.3	12.3	12.8
Japan	33.2	35.3	37.3	38.4	37.5	34.7	34.8
Small Industrial	17.5	19.1	18.0	20.4	20.4	22.5	22.3
Other Western Europe	1.7	1.6	1.4	2.6	2.5	2.7	2.6
Australasia	0.6	0.6	0.6	0.5	0.5	0.7	0.7
Newly Industrializing Countries	15.3	16.9	16.0	17.3	17.3	19.2	19.0
Third World	1.8	2.4	2.1	4.1	4.0	5.2	5.2
Latin America	0.3	0.9	0.7	0.8	0.8	1.4	1.4
South Asia	1.2	1.2	1.0	1.2	1.2	1.5	1.5
West Asia	0.3	0.3	0.5	2.0	2.0	2.3	2.3
ASEAN	5.7	5.8	5.4	4.3	4.0	4.6	4.8
Indonesia	0.2	0.2	—	—	—	—	—
Malaysia	3.7	3.9	3.6	2.6	2.6	2.8	2.8
Singapore	1.1	1.1	1.3	1.2	1.0	1.3	1.5
Philippines	0.7	0.6	0.5	0.5	0.5	0.5	0.5
Not Specified	12.5	9.8	9.0	8.6	8.5	5.0	5.0
Total	100	100	100	100	100	100	100
Geographical Dispersion Index	42.5	44.2	45.2	45.8	45.5	44.7	44.7
Annual Growth Rate (percentage)	—	2.6	10.1	18.7	4.2	−9.1	4.5

* 1974 as of January 31; 1976 as of June 30; 1978 as of March 31; all others as of December 31.

possible exception of Thailand. Bangkok's dependence on Japan remains quite pronounced.

This brief discussion of economic security would be incomplete without some assessment of ASEAN's growing apprehension over Japan's economic dominance in the region. One problem looming on the horizon for ASEAN is the increased importance of China as a trade competitor for Japanese markets and capital. ASEAN leaders have already begun to complain that Japan has been willing to commit billions of yen to Chinese projects sight unseen, while any large-scale investment for ASEAN is delayed pending elaborate feasibility studies. Japan has been willing to purchase raw materials and semiprocessed goods from China at prices above the world market in order to obtain future contracts—a tactic the ASEAN states have been unable to employ.[62]

Japanese analysts acknowledge this differential treatment of Beijing, explaining it in terms of China's greater political importance. This reasoning sees ASEAN almost entirely in business terms and does not take it seriously from a political standpoint. Japanese business is less concerned about profit return from China, but invests in ASEAN strictly on the basis of commercial considerations. Moreover, Japan's reluctance to help the ASEAN states develop entrepreneurial skills through technology transfer and managerial training may be explained by the enthnocentrism of Japanese business. Japanese businessmen, accustomed to lifetime loyalty on the part of their personnel, are loath to train foreign nationals or provide trade secrets for fear that these skills will then benefit rivals when host country managerial personnel leave for other positions.[63] Rather, Japanese businessmen prefer local Chinese as host country partners, particularly if the Japanese company is manufacturing products strictly for the local market. Host country Chinese generally specialize in marketing and are essentially uninterested in the production process.

Franklin Weinstein has summarized Southeast Asia's economic growth challenge in the following terms:

> Development, then, is not merely a matter of industrialization or the acquisition of wealth; it involves as well the creation of institutions capable, on a self-sustaining basis, of channeling resources into more productive uses and distributing the output of that process to the populace in a way that will win sufficiently diffuse support to maintain the system. This means, among other things, the establishment of a bureaucracy which can be relied on to implement policies with a reasonable degree of consistency; the cultivation of a broad base of entrepreneurial, managerial, and technical skill; development of a capacity to raise capital internally

through an effective tax system; and, most pressing given the seriousness of the employment problem, the creation of jobs that will enable the majority of the populace not only to survive but to be productive.[64]

None of the political, strategic, and economic issues challenging the autonomy and viability of the ASEAN states in the 1980s is easily resolved. All are formidable. The past two decades in Southeast Asia have demonstrated a certain advantage in multilateral diplomacy as a device for negotiating with both outsiders and adversaries on a more equal basis. ASEAN's future depends on the continuing skill of the five to deter opponents and elicit supporters' assistance while rejecting the latters' control. The remainder of this study assesses ASEAN's successes and failures and projects possible futures for this prominent Third World regional group. ASEAN's performance in the 1980s, if successful, could provide a model for other Third World regions. Many are watching.

2 | CHALLENGES FACING *ASEAN*

Conflicts Among the Membership

Among ASEAN's more tangible achievements has been the creation of consultative processes to ameliorate conflicts within the Association membership. Throughout the 1960s, the region was characterized by high tension resulting from border demarcation conflicts (Malaysia-Indonesia), border insurgency control concerns (Malaysia-Indonesia, Malaysia-Thailand, Malaysia-Philippines), the Philippine claim to Sabah initiated in 1962, and Singapore's expulsion from Malaysia (1965). It is noteworthy that none of these serious challenges to regional peace remains a major obstacle to ASEAN cooperation today—despite periodic reports of continued Malaysian assistance to the Moro rebels in the southern Philippines.

ASEAN mediation over Sabah proved so successful that the procedure was written into the treaties on settlement of intra-ASEAN conflict signed at the Bali Summit of 1976. At the Kuala Lumpur Summit in 1977, President Marcos—in the ASEAN spirit—announced that the Philippines would withdraw its claim to Sabah. (Although the Philippine government delayed fulfilling this pledge, primarily because of domestic considerations, it let the Sabah issue remain dormant.) In effect, nationalism was muted in the name of regionalism. Nevertheless, Marcos could revive the claim if it appeared that Malaysia was becoming involved once again in supporting the Muslim rebels by smuggling arms and offering sanctuary.[1]

An impasse appears to exist over the Moro Rebellion/Sabah claim issue. Both Kuala Lumpur and Manila are interested ultimately in the creation of a border security agreement that could effectively control smuggling and drug-running. Such an agreement could be modeled after the Thai-Malaysian border accord, complete with hot-pursuit provisions. Marcos has reportedly insisted, however, that in return for Manila's abrogation of the Sabah claim, there should be not only a joint border security arrangement but concerted Malaysian assistance to starve out the Filipino rebels, some 140,000 of whom may be in Sabah (15 percent of its population). Malaysia cannot agree to any such plan because it is a Muslim nation, and it has let the Philippines know that there can be no joint border arrangement while the Sabah claim still exists.[2]

As representatives of the Islamic Conference, Malaysia and Indonesia encourage the Moros and the Philippine government to negotiate a peaceful settlement on the basis of the 1976 Tripoli agreement— "within the framework of respect for the territorial integrity and sovereignty of the Philippines."[3] Thus, ASEAN ties have superseded religious preference, as two of the Philippines' Muslim neighbors serve virtually as Manila's spokesmen in international Muslim forums. This is particularly remarkable for Malaysia, where Muslim sentiment is strong. To defend the Philippine position entails some internal political price for the ruling Alliance party, which it apparently is willing to pay for ASEAN solidarity.

A dramatic indication of the remarkable degree of harmony within ASEAN at the turn of the decade is that the Sabah/Moro Rebellion dispute is the only significant potentially disruptive conflict within ASEAN. Compared with the mid-1960s when every member had at least one outstanding dispute with another, many of which had led to armed confrontation, the increase in amity and reduction in tension is more prominent than in any other world region.

There remain, nonetheless, occasional lower-level conflicts that are resolved by bilateral or trilateral negotiations. For example, the joint claims of Indonesia and Malaysia to the Strait of Malacca leave Singapore unenthusiastic since its role as a global trader could be jeopardized should its neighbors attempt to close the strait. But Kuala Lumpur's and Jakarta's acknowledgment that the great powers have "legitimate interests" in the maintenance of open sea-lanes between the Indian Ocean and South China Sea mollified Singapore's worries. Indeed, Malaysia originally adopted the national waters concept to accommodate Indonesia's strategic position in the aftermath of Indonesia's confrontation with Malaysia (1963–1965).[4] For Indonesia, this posture signifies both its implicit claim to regional leadership and its adherence to nonalignment while it courts Western capital and follows economic policies of the World Bank and the International Monetary Fund. It is, then, a device to balance growing economic dependence on the West by underlining its political independence with respect to territorial integrity. Singapore understands the symbolic value of the Malacca Strait statement to both Indonesia and Malaysia and has been willing to accommodate them.

Parallel to its claim to the Malacca Strait, Indonesia (along with the Philippines) has also asserted an "archipelago principle," beginning in 1958 at the first U.N. Law of the Sea Conference. This principle defines territorial waters by

> drawing imaginary straight lines between the outermost points of the country's outermost islands, and then territorial waters and economic zones are measured from their baseline. Thus Indonesia swiftly laid claim to over 660,000 square miles of ocean and thereby sought to encapsulate within its own national waters such important straits used for international navigation as Sunda, Lombok, and Makassar. The principal factor immediately impelling this declaration seems to have been the occurrence of armed dissidence and revolt against the central government from the "Outer Islands" —a long established Java-centric designation. Thus, at a time when the authority of the Javanese-based government seemed likely to crumble was asserted a defiant definition of the unity and integrity of the archipelagic state and its adjacent waters.[5]

Malaysia was more than a little concerned about Indonesia's declaration since it could cut access between Malaya and Sarawak and Sabah. The two sides reached an understanding in 1976. In exchange for supporting Indonesia's archipelago concept, Malaysia would be granted historical rights, including undisturbed air and sea passage between west and east Malaysia. In early 1982, a treaty embodying these principles was initialed. Moreover, the negotiating text of the current Law of the Sea Conference on mid-ocean archipelagos would also protect Malaysian access and fishing rights.[6]

Other law of the sea developments are also complicating ASEAN relations. On March 21, 1980, Indonesian President Suharto formally declared an exclusive 200-mile economic zone for water and seabed exploitation. Seven of Indonesia's neighbors have declared similar zones: Australia, Vietnam, Cambodia, Japan, Papua New Guinea, Burma, and the Philippines. Suharto's declaration will require negotiation of median boundaries with four of these countries as well as with Malaysia, which has not yet formalized its claim to an economic zone. These are not considered onerous issues, however. Thailand and Malaysia, for example, had little difficulty in reaching an agreement marking the territorial sea boundary between their two countries with respect to the continental shelf in the Gulf of Thailand and South China Sea. The two states will share seabed exploitation of one unresolved area as part of their overall border region development cooperation.[7]

Minor disputes over small islands exist between Singapore and Malaysia and the Philippines and Malaysia. Authorities on all sides have indicated willingness to negotiate settlements.[8]

The most amicable and mutually advantageous resolution of a bilateral border problem was the Thai-Malaysian agreement to cooperate against Malayan Communist Party (MCP) insurgents who took refuge in southern Thailand and to a smaller degree against Thai Muslim irredentists who were obtaining assistance from co-religionists across the Malaysian border. Up through the mid-1970s, this issue had disturbed the generally good relations between the two governments. In 1976, nationalist reaction in Thailand to a Malaysian hot-pursuit operation on Thai territory almost led to an abrogation of the border control agreement. Subsequent talks, however, actually led to a strengthened border accord in March 1977, which expanded hot-pursuit activities. It is generally understood that Malaysia will discourage support for Thai separatists in return for Thailand's cooperation in controlling the MCP remnants. Neither side wishes to see the other's problem totally eliminated, however, for fear that the latter's incentive for further cooperation would be attenuated.[9]

Limited Military Capabilities

Despite notable progress in settling interstate differences, ASEAN's military and security operations both within the Association's boundaries or adjacent to them are hampered politically and militarily. First and foremost, ASEAN has argued that its security cannot be assured by indigenous military means. Security will grow out of successful national and regional economic development. This emphasis on the economic bases of security has led to a de-emphasis within ASEAN on formal military establishments. (See Table 16.) Thus, Indonesia—the biggest and most important of the ASEAN states—has deliberately starved its armed forces, especially the navy and airforce, of scarce foreign exchange. Even more striking is the fact that the combined military strength of the ASEAN five cannot match Vietnam's (although, of course, the SRV must deploy a significant number of its forces toward China).

TABLE 16
ASEAN AND INDOCHINA: SOME INDICES

	Population (millions)	Armed Forces (thousands)	Forces as Percentage of Men 18–45	Paramilitary Forces (in thousands)	Estimated GNP (millions)	Estimated Defense Expenditures (millions)	GNP per capita†	
							Amount 1977	Real Growth Rate, 1970–1977 (percentage)
Vietnam	50.3	1,020	10.8	1,570.0	8,600	n.a.	n.a.	n.a.
Laos	3.4	48.5	n.a.	n.a.	210 (1978)	29 (1977–78)	90	n.a.
Cambodia	6.0	*	n.a.	n.a.	n.a.	n.a.	n.a.	n.a.
Thailand	46.5	216	2.5	66.0	21,700 (1978)	940 (1979–80)	430	4.1
Malaysia	13.3	64.5	2.5	213.0	14,700 (1978)	693 (1978)	970	4.9
Singapore	2.4	36	6.4	37.5	7,540 (1978)	410 (1977–78)	2,820	6.6
Indonesia	150.0	239	0.9	112.0	22,600 (1977)	1,470 (1979–80)	320	5.7
Philippines	47.7	103	1.1	82.0	23,200 (1978)	793 (1978)	460	3.7

SOURCE: International Institute of Strategic Studies, *The Military Balance, 1979–80* (London, 1981), pp. 66–74, 97.

NOTE: All monetary values are given in U.S.$ equivalents.

*"The former Khmer Liberation Army had about 12 divisions before the invasion by Vietnam in December 1978. The country is now occupied by 20 Vietnamese divisions (approximately 180,000 troops)." (IISS, *The Military Balance, 1979–80*, p. 67.)

† Data from World Bank Atlas, 1979.

There have been voices in ASEAN urging the creation of a stronger military capability—particularly in Singapore and in Indonesian military circles. Indonesian Defense Minister Maraden Panggabean, after assisting in the expansion of bilateral mutual defense operations with Malaysia in 1975, suggested that "other ASEAN nations should establish defense cooperation on the Malaysia-Indonesia pattern."[10] The 1976 Bali Summit endorsed bilateral military cooperation among ASEAN members. Indonesia even raised the possibility of a joint ASEAN military force at the foreign ministers' conference in 1977 after Thailand had expressed its hope for ASEAN help in case of external aggression. The meeting did not endorse the idea, however.[11] The prevailing view maintained—at least until the 1979 Vietnamese invasion of Cambodia—that ASEAN's security concerns involved border insurgencies and that these could be handled through bilateral cooperation. The Malaysian-Thai and Indonesian-Malaysian arrangements were cited as both successful and sufficient. There was no need for ASEAN as an organization to become "tainted" with military responsibilities recalling those of the moribund SEATO. Moreover, by coping with regional security problems in an ad hoc bilateral fashion, ASEAN could reassure its communist neighbors that the Association's activities were peaceful and confined to economic transactions from which the PRC, Indochina, and even the Soviet Union could also benefit.

The practical problems involved have reinforced this lack of political will to create a joint defense. There are virtually no common weapons systems among the ASEAN states. Military doctrine, training, logistics, and languages vary from one state to another. Moreover, the stationing of mixed contingents on the territory of any given member to cope with an insurgency could be a politically hazardous venture.[12] Even the Malaysian border-crossing operations into Thailand against the MCP remnants elicit periodic remonstrations from local elites concerning the treatment of villages suspected of assisting the guerrillas.

By downgrading any regional military threats, the ASEAN states have devoted only minimal resources to their defense establishments. The best example, once again, is Indonesia, whose military is the largest among Association members but also the least prepared to engage in major military action. The country's air and naval equipment, originally acquired from the Soviet Union in the early 1960s, has run down without significant replacement. In a country composed of thousands of islands, the lack of naval and air capability is something of a paradox, given Jakarta's insistence on the archipelagic principle of territorial waters and control of the Malacca Strait. In these instances, symbolic politics and military capabilities are not mutually reinforcing.

Since 1966, Indonesia's military budget has been only about 2 percent of GNP. It actually fell below that percentage in the late 1970s. Army battalions are understrength, poorly equipped, and frequently ill trained. The suppression of separatist forces in East Timor in the mid-1970s exhausted most of the small-arms ammunition inventory, which means that recent military maneuvers were conducted without live ammunition.[13] In an attempt to remedy this situation, Defense Minister General Mohamed Jusuf has embarked on a program to upgrade 50 of the army's 90 battalions to a high standard of training and equipment. Since this effort began only in 1981, it is too early to determine either its success or its impact on Indonesia's *regional* military capability. Since the army's primary mission is domestic, however, with a noncommissioned officer stationed in every village, it is unlikely that even the enhanced military General Jusuf envisages would have much of a role outside the home islands. An attempt to move forces any distance beyond Indonesia would severely strain its air- and sea-lift capability. On the other hand, Indonesia began in 1981 to expand its naval base on Natuna Island in the South China Sea—a potentially petroleum-rich area currently being disputed by Vietnam.

The military is undoubtedly benefiting along with other government sectors from windfall oil profits. Thus, its 1980–81 budget of U.S. $2.1 billion is 43 percent higher than the previous year's $1.47 billion. But the military's percentage share of the total budget continues to decline, underlining its persistently low priority. While the national budget more than doubled between 1975 and 1980 (from $8.4 billion to $16.9 billion), official military spending has increased only by 68 percent, leading to a steady decline in its share of the budget from 14.7 percent in 1977–78 to 12.5 percent in 1980–81.[14]

These facts suggest that Indonesia's leaders are relatively unconcerned about either a direct external threat to its security or even an indirect threat through an attack on Thailand. There are several possible explanations for this relative complacency. Indonesian leaders may not view the regional environment as militarily threatening. They may not believe that a threat to Thailand affects Indonesia's security since the latter is an archipelago and not attached to mainland Southeast Asia. Or they may calculate that in the event of a threat to Indonesia, Jakarta lacks the military wherewithal to cope with a direct confrontation and must seek a modus vivendi through diplomacy and a search for outside guarantees in the event of major war. The latter interpretation is given some credence by reports of Indonesia's role in persuading President Marcos to negotiate a new treaty for U.S. bases in the Philippines on terms acceptable to the Americans.[15] By keeping U.S. forces deployed in East Asia, Indonesia (and other ASEAN states) acquire a deterrent against possible adversaries and a potential ally in the event of war. This, in turn, permits something of a military "free ride" since defense budgets can remain relatively low if governments believe they can rely on outside aid in the event of a regional crisis.

While Indonesia's military posture signifies the security concerns of ASEAN's largest member (some would also say the Association's self-designated leader), Thailand's represents that of the Association's "front-line" state. If any ASEAN member is going to become directly involved in military hostilities with Vietnam, it will be Thailand. Thus, an examination of Thailand's military capability should provide a reasonably good picture of how the most beleaguered noncommunist state in Southeast Asia views its security environment.

Thailand's army numbers 145,000; the majority are dispersed in counterinsurgency activities in the south, central, north, and northeast regions of the country. The last two regions, adjacent to Laos, have raised irredentist fears for years because of their demographic character (heavily Laotian and hill tribe), their economic condition (poor subsistence farming, opium, and slash-and-burn agriculture), and their vulnerability to Thai communist insurgents who received succor and sanctuary in Laos. Now added to this perennial territorial concern in the north is Thailand's eastern land border down to the Gulf of Siam. Since January 1979, Cambodia, too, has been occupied by Vietnamese forces, with approximately 100,000 deployed along the Thai border in 1981.

New tanks and TOW (tube-launched, optically tracked, wire-guided) and Dragon antitank missiles have been ordered from the United States to improve the military's insignificant armored capabilities. The air force, too, has only a limited defensive clout, with 35 F-5 interceptors and no specialized aircraft to interdict at a distance. In fact, the main mission of the air force has been to assist the army's counterinsurgency activities rather than to engage either enemy air power or conventional ground forces. In sum, while the Thai military cooperates reasonably effectively in cross-border operations with its Malaysian counterpart to control small-scale insurgencies, it is not a fighting force designed, equipped, or trained to take on one of the finest military institutions in Asia—the Vietnamese People's Army (VPA).[16] Some U.S. observers are particularly pessimistic about Thai military capabilities in any one-to-one confrontation, and note in particular the lack of troop discipline, incompetence among some of the senior officer ranks, and disorganized command-and-control procedures.[17]

The new Vietnamese threat has led to some increase in defense expenditures. Even before the Cambodian invasion, Thai officials beefed up the defense budget by almost 16 percent for fiscal 1979, compared with the previous year, and raised it another 15 percent in 1982 over 1981. Nevertheless, this is all fairly inconsequential—Vietnam's army still outnumbers that of Thailand four to one. The VPA has 900 Soviet-built tanks compared with Thailand's 150 Korean War–vintage machines (although new American models were beginning to arrive in late 1981).[18] The key point is that any serious effort by Thailand to catch up militarily with Vietnam would undermine the former's economic development program, which, in turn, would fuel another sort of threat—this one perhaps more dangerous because domestic strife directly rends the social fabric. Lee Kwan Yew summed up Thailand's military situation and that of ASEAN more generally when he stated that the region's military forces are committed to coping with insurgencies and that "there is no combination of forces in Southeast Asia that can stop the Vietnamese on the mainland of Asia."[19]

The author's interviews with knowledgeable analysts in the ASEAN countries in the summer of 1979, during the height of the "boat people" exodus, and again in 1981 elicited pessimistic assessments of the possibility of any joint ASEAN military action. Responses emphasized across-the-board insufficiencies among ASEAN forces and that very little in the way of military aid could be given by any of the members to Thailand since their own military forces were unsophisticated and undersupplied. Joint military operations were even further from reality. There was no common language, doctrine, or equipment standardization among the five. ASEAN military forces had no experience—real or simulated—in fighting on one another's soil. One respondent commented wryly that an Indonesian unit landing in the Thai jungle would promptly get lost. He then recounted comparable experiences during the Konfrontasi with Malaysia under Sukarno.

During the 1970s, then, the ASEAN states did not radically increase military spending despite the American defeat in Indochina and the concomitant rise of Vietnam to the status of major regional power. Instead, there was general agreement that security threats to the area lay in domestic insurgencies, frequently in inhospitable border regions between states. To cope with these disturbances, ASEAN members developed bilateral cooperation and small-unit counterinsurgency warfare. They did not seek to equip themselves with expensive armor, air power, or major sea-going ocean craft. Indeed, Thailand and Malaysia entered into some cooperative small arms–manufacturing arrangements, which they hoped would lead to self-sufficiency.[20] Joint ASEAN military cooperation against a conventional aggressor has been neither contemplated, anticipated, nor planned.

However, once Thailand confronted a conventional military threat on its eastern border, earlier military plans for insurgency control became essentially irrelevant; and the ramifications spread beyond Thailand. In Malaysia, for example, highly mobile strike forces trained to deal with MCP guerrillas became overstretched along the Thai-Malaysian border when Thailand moved some of its 4th Army to the Cambodian border. This development further extended an already thinly spread Malaysian military, many of whose units had already been assigned to watch the long east coast for boat refugees.[21]

There is concern in ASEAN capitals that a direct military conflict between Thailand and Vietnam, for example, over the disposition of Cambodian refugees could involve other members. Security obligations are ambiguous; some leaders appear to call for greater participation on Thailand's behalf, while others fear precisely such a development. Thus, President Marcos has urged Vietnam not to press Thailand militarily over the border situation, for to do so might mean that the rest of ASEAN would be obliged to aid Bangkok. Malaysia has adopted a similar position, although it is stated more positively. The chairman of Indonesia's Parliamentary Commission for Foreign Affairs urged that ASEAN troops be sent to the Thai-Cambodian border—a proposal rejected almost immediately by the Indonesian Foreign Office.[22]

Thailand itself has chosen not to call for ASEAN military support, but it did request that U.N. civilian observers be placed along the border to insure security in the "displaced persons camps" and to guarantee adequate distribution of food and medicine.[23] Behind this appeal is the hope that international observers would deter VPA raids on the border camps and provide legitimacy for aid to Cambodian resistance groups camped along the border.

By 1981, Thailand, Indonesia, and Malaysia had significantly expanded their defense budgets—the latter two with oil profits and the former with the assistance of U.S. foreign military credit sales. Nevertheless, plans for these enhanced military forces remained essentially unchanged, with the bulk of the new resources going to ground and air forces—the latter beefed up for ground support missions through the acquisition of additional A-4s. It is noteworthy that although U.S. experts consider the A-4 a reliable counterinsurgency weapon, they believe it incapable of engaging in effective air-to-air combat or of projecting force beyond national borders.

External Challenges to ASEAN

The Vietnamese (and Soviet) Threat

ASEAN's inability to meet a direct, conventional military attack on its membership with only the Association's military resources is obvious. Clearly, any reduction in the military dimension of external threats to ASEAN and increase in its diplomatic options will enhance the Association's ability to cope with a threatening environment.

Since 1978, Southeast Asian politics have changed radically. The catalyst, as in the past, has been conflict on the Indochina peninsula. Vietnam's decision to establish military and political hegemony in Indochina and its new alliance with the USSR added another dimension to the Sino-Vietnamese contest for regional dominance—namely, the Sino-Soviet conflict. Vietnam's decision to move westward led to the re-establishment of a war economy within the country, which, in turn, caused Hanoi to expel those whom it saw as either troublemakers or potential fifth columnists on China's behalf. The result was the hundreds of thousands of refugees streaming by both land and sea into the ASEAN states and in turn threatening their racial balance and social stability. By 1980, ASEAN faced a difficult political problem: how to maintain neutrality in the Sino-Vietnam and Sino-Soviet disputes, while backing Thailand against Vietnamese pressure neither to support nor to repatriate several hundred thousand refugees. Vietnam viewed the camps along the Cambodian-Thai border as manpower bases for anti-Vietnamese Cambodian insurgencies. In an implicit effort to maintain its independence and territorial integrity, Thailand adopted a policy that happened to parallel China's. This appeared to place Bangkok (and by extension, ASEAN) on the PRC side of both the Sino-Vietnam and Sino-Soviet conflicts and seemed to undermine ASEAN's stated posture of neutrality. Almost a decade of diplomacy was unraveling as refugees fled ahead of almost 200,000 VPA regulars. ASEAN was being sucked into a new maelstrom.

These new challenges also stimulated political coordination within ASEAN. Attempts to split the Association's united front, beginning with SRV Premier Pham Van Dong's visits in 1978, led the ASEAN heads of state to agree to coordinate their positions on Indochina. Thus, Dong's tour yielded identical communiqués from each capital he visited, a virtually unprecedented development for ASEAN.

Of course, Vietnam's suspicion of ASEAN is well-founded. Its members did, after all, back the losing side in the second Indochina war, and Thailand was directly involved in the fighting against communist forces throughout the peninsula. Vietnam may well perceive ASEAN as allied with its current enemies since it was associated with Hanoi's previous adversaries.

Vietnam, for its part, gave ASEAN sufficient cause for worry not long after it gained control of the south. An authoritative *Nhan Dan* editorial (February 28, 1976) proclaimed that "the victories of the Vietnamese, Cambodians and Lao peoples have had the effect of setting forth the Southeast Asian peoples' struggle for independence and freedom as an example and has strongly stimulated this struggle." It went on to exhort these revolutionary forces:

> The struggle of the Southeast Asian peoples is enjoying favorable conditions and has the brightest prospects ever seen in their history of the past century. By intensifying this struggle, the peoples of the Southeast Asian countries will certainly foil all neocolonialist schemes and tricks of the U.S. imperialists and reactionaries, restore true national independence and sovereignty and restore the ownership of the Southeast Asian region to the Southeast Asians.[24]

Hanoi's behavior at the Nonaligned Conference that summer in Colombo, especially its and Vientiane's condemnation of ZOPFAN as a mask for renewed Western intervention, reinforced ASEAN apprehensions. This was followed in 1977 by the SRV-Lao Treaty of Friendship and Cooperation, Articles Two and Five of which could be interpreted as a charter for intervention in support of the "people's struggle" in Southeast Asia.[25]

Thailand was particularly exercised by this aggressive rhetoric, for Laos could justify irredentist claims to sixteen provinces in north and northeast Thailand and Cambodia to eight others in eastern Thailand. Should a Vietnam-controlled Indochina choose to press these claims, Bangkok could do little to halt them.

Vietnam modified its belligerence toward ASEAN in 1978 as a prelude to its December–January 1978–79 invasion of Cambodia. The SRV hoped to neutralize ASEAN hostility and perhaps split the Association by proving that some of its members (Malaysia and Indonesia) viewed China as a greater long-term threat then they did Vietnam. Moreover, in 1976 Hanoi established diplomatic relations with the Philippines during Phan Hien's visit. Each side agreed that its territory would not be used as a base for "direct or indirect aggression and intervention against the other country."[26] Other reports that the SRV had been refusing to provide arms from its huge captured American inventory to regional insurgencies seemed reassuring.[27]

The modus vivendi that might have been arranged with ASEAN fell apart in November 1978, when Vietnam signed what amounted to a security treaty with the USSR. In the space of two signatures, ASEAN's hopes for regional neutralization evaporated, the USSR became a major factor in Southeast Asian security, and the Sino-Soviet conflict intruded into ASEAN-Vietnamese relations.

Thailand was particularly alarmed about the Soviet-Vietnamese treaty because of the pattern of events that had followed previous agreements between the USSR and the SRV: political stalemates had been overcome by military force. There were the Tet offensives of 1968 and 1972 and the sweeping military victory of 1975. This time Hanoi's invasion of Cambodia followed shortly after the signing of the treaty. The SRV-Soviet treaty coincided with Hanoi's announcement of a Cambodian Liberation Front on Vietnamese soil. The subsequent military occupation of Cambodia in the front's name boded ill for Thai security. Analysts in Bangkok reasoned that Hanoi could create a parallel liberation movement for Thailand's northeast and, with Soviet supplies, expand westward.[28]

In one sense, the Soviets may be boxed into backing Vietnam's military designs. Article Six of the treaty requires each party to aid the other in the event of an attack. The SRV could engage Thai forces and then claim Thai aggression had occurred, attempting to invoke Russian assistance. Actual Soviet involvement might not even be necessary. The very possibility of Russian involvement could, in turn, discourage other ASEAN members and possibly even the United States from significantly countering Hanoi's move.

On the other hand, Soviet and Vietnamese goals may not be entirely consonant. The USSR, after all, must have a global policy, while Vietnam's concerns need not extend beyond the region. Well into 1977, for example, the SRV consciously established political distance between itself and the Soviet Union. It did not accept the Soviet view, prevailing at that time, that ASEAN was an imperialist creation.[29] Nor did it support the Soviet proposal for an Asian collective security treaty. Furthermore, much to Russia's displeasure, Hanoi opted for membership in the World Bank.[30]

Pham Van Dong attempted to establish a foreign policy that transcended the old Hanoi-Moscow-Beijing triangle by creating new links with the West and Third World. In foreign aid, for example, he hoped that the socialist countries would provide 50 percent of the funds needed, with the other half coming from the United States, Canada, Western Europe, and Japan. He was particularly interested in American oil technology.

In the spring of 1977, the SRV promulgated a liberal foreign investment code, which included provisions for joint enterprises and wholly owned foreign projects in special export industries. Tax concessions were generous, and the right to repatriate profits was given. The moderates in the VCP seemed to be in the ascendance, paralleling the situation in the PRC where the Gang of Four had been overthrown in 1976.

American officials still claimed that Congress would not approve economic assistance for Vietnam. The Vietnamese made one last effort in the summer of 1978 to mollify the Americans by dropping demands for reparations or aid and indicating they would accept simply an establishment of diplomatic relations. This total capitulation went unheeded by the Carter administration. Pham Van Dong then traveled to Europe to find alternative financing, only to be rebuffed with the argument that the Europeans awaited normalization of Vietnamese relations with the United States. Dong returned to a serious situation. Vietnam was facing a drought. Reconstruction work had bogged down. Earlier, in April 1978, Cambodia had launched large-scale attacks along the border, further diverting Vietnam's attention from reconstruction.

By the time Dong went to Moscow in June 1978, he had nowhere else to turn. The Soviets took a characteristically hard line, insisting that Hanoi align with it. In Beijing Dong also found intransigence, partly because of his trip to Moscow and partly because of the Cambodian conflict. China would give no additional aid and refused to discuss the Spratly and Paracel islands dispute. Moreover, the PRC was openly backing the Pol Pot regime's aggressive behavior on the Vietnamese border, with the aim of preventing Hanoi's consolidation of an Indochinese sphere of control by supporting an anti-Vietnamese Cambodia.

In fact, as early as September 1977, Hanoi's Politburo had apparently decided that Soviet aid was essential to consolidate the SRV's domestic gains and to meet the Cambodian border threat. With Soviet backing, a counterattack was launched against Cambodia. At the same time, the velvet glove came off with respect to collectivization in the south with a brutal campaign bearing all the earmarks of direction from the Stalinist Truong Chinh. Bourgeois elements in the cities were the most harshly squeezed. Most of these were Vietnamese of Chinese descent. Given the choice of moving to the New Economic Zones along the Cambodian frontier or buying their way out of the country in small craft, many opted for the latter.

By the end of 1978, Vietnam had not only become a full member of COMECON (its only Asian communist component, excepting the Mongolian People's Republic), but it had also signed a de facto security treaty with Moscow. The moderate strategy had atrophied, and Vietnam became a full-fledged member of the Soviet bloc. Two pro-Soviet military men, Defense Minister Vo Nguyen Giap and Army Chief of Staff Von Tien Dung, were promoted to prime minister and minister of defense, respectively.

Any analysis of Hanoi's decision to abandon its moderate strategy must apportion some of the responsibility to the hard-line policies of both China and the United States. Their refusal to provide reconstruction assistance, combined with Beijing's efforts to destabilize the Cambodian-Vietnamese border region, strengthened the political position of those Vietnamese leaders who urged an alignment with the USSR.

Concomitant with the Soviet-Vietnam Treaty of Friendship and Cooperation, Moscow undertook both a massive military resupply of the VPA as well as the responsibility of underwriting the SRV's economic viability. Moscow was providing up to 30 percent of Vietnam's rice in late 1979. Other vital commodities from the USSR included petroleum, chemical fertilizers, and spare parts for the SRV's transportation system. COMECON has provided preferential exchange rates for intrabloc trade and has picked up some of the aid projects abandoned by China. And, of critical military importance, Moscow has provided AN-12 transport planes to ferry men and supplies into Cambodia to sustain the presence of close to 200,000 VPA forces there.[31] Vietnamese trade with the Soviet Union rose from $702.1 million to $910.7 million in 1979, but imports exceeded exports by $459.9 million, compared with $234.9 million in 1978.[32]

While Vietnam views its treaty with the Soviet Union as a necessity to sustain its bid for control of Indochina against China and possibly a U.S.-backed ASEAN, the USSR sees it in a larger context. Moscow's willingness to underwrite Vietnam's adventure in Cambodia and Laos is part of a larger scheme traceable to its heretofore unsuccessful bid for a series of bilateral arrangements that could be consolidated into an Asian collective security pact. Originally broached in 1969, the concept aborted because no Asian country was willing to antagonize China gratuitously. Even India, which signed a treaty of cooperation with the USSR in 1971 for its own anti-Pakistani purposes, carefully emphasized that the pact did not alter Delhi's nonaligned policy. When, however, Japan and China concluded a friendship accord containing an implied anti-Soviet objective (the antihegemony clause) and that treaty paved the way for China's modernization with Japanese assistance, Soviet policymakers revived the Asian collective security idea as a counterbalance to what they perceived to be the creation of a Sino-Japanese-U.S. axis. The Soviet-Vietnamese treaty would confront China with the prospect of a two-front war, somewhat diluting any future military buildup that might grow out of Japanese and American assistance for the PRC's modernization.

As noted above, the price Moscow has paid for the alliance has not been inexpensive. By 1981, Soviet assistance was estimated to be running up to $6 million per day, and over 5,000 Russian technicians were located throughout Vietnam.[33] The USSR's heavy subsidy, however, should provide Moscow with some leverage over time, particularly if Vietnam seems unable to consolidate its position in Cambodia and continues to alienate ASEAN. The USSR could exert some influence upon Hanoi for moderation. Moscow has, for example, promised that Vietnam will not invade Thailand. Indeed, both Moscow and Hanoi denied the VPA border incursions into Thailand in June 1980, allowing them to continue to claim that this pledge was still intact. ASEAN's ability to counter such incursions is virtually nil. An Indonesian Foreign Ministry official, for example, speculated that if Vietnam invaded Thailand, Indonesia might close the Strait of Malacca to Russian shipping, but at the same time he acknowledged that Jakarta would not attempt to interdict Soviet vessels physically.[34]

Analysts in the ASEAN states interviewed by the author in the summer of 1979 seemed relatively sanguine that Vietnam would not attempt to repeat its Cambodian operation in Thailand. Two reasons were most often cited: (1) that Vietnam was already overextended, given its administrative responsibilities for itself, Laos, and Cambodia; and (2) that Vietnam had not created a viable puppet, comparable to the Cambodian Liberation Front, that could be used as a political facade to mask an invasion of Thailand. Moreover, historically Vietnam's sphere of influence has not extended beyond Indochina. Also, neither Vietnam nor the Soviet Union has the ability to foment revolution within the ASEAN states, whose communist parties are all dominated by pro-Beijing elements.

ASEAN remains concerned, nevertheless, at the Soviet-SRV potential for fostering and abetting "liberation movements" on their territories. Moscow still publicizes their successes, giving the incumbent governments an uneasy feeling. Typical is the *Pravda* comment, "The successes of the liberation struggle of the peoples of Kampuchea, Iran, Afghanistan, Ethiopia and a number of other countries cogently shows the direction in which the development of world events is moving. 'It is only the opponents of progress,' Comrade L. I. Brezhnev has pointed out, 'who refuse to see that these changes spring up on national soils.'"[35]

When Pham Van Dong visited Thailand, Indonesia, and the Philippines in September 1978, he attempted to reassure each government that the SRV would not engage in subversion.[36] In a sense, these pledges were relatively costless, given the traditional pro-Chinese orientation of communist guerrillas in all three. These assurances were almost wholly discounted, however, when Vietnam marched into Cambodia in January 1979. Since that time relations between ASEAN and Hanoi could be most aptly characterized as "diplomatically belligerent." That already tense status deteriorated even further, however, in June 1980, when in response to Thai repatriation of Cambodian refugees, the VPA crossed the border and scattered some 200,000 refugees who had been loosely controlled by anti-Vietnamese Cambodian guerrillas.

Earlier, Vietnamese Foreign Minister Nguyen Co Thach had warned that the SRV might use force if Thailand continued to assist the Khmer Rouge resistance. Military analysts believe that the resistance cannot be eliminated unless Vietnam engages in hot pursuit across the Thai border. The VPA refrained from doing so until Thailand began to engage in the large-scale repatriation of Cambodians (over 8,000, though most were women and children) into Khmer Rouge–controlled territory.[37] At that point, the VPA attacked, probably hoping to achieve several ends: (1) the dispersion of refugees deeper into Thailand and away from Khmer Rouge control; (2) the disruption of the international food distribution program along the Thai border, which was drawing tens of thousands of Cambodians away from the government in Phnom Penh as well as providing food for the Khmer Rouge; and (3) a warning to Thailand not to continue assisting the Khmer Rouge, given Bangkok's military vulnerability.

The Refugee Issue

The greatest human tragedy growing out of Vietnam's treatment of ethnic Chinese throughout Indochina and the crushing failures of Cambodia's harvests in the late 1970s has been the extraordinary addition to Southeast Asia's already heavy refugee population. Refugees are not a new phenomenon in the region.[38] During the first Indochina war (1945–1954) several tens of thousands of Vietnamese settled in Thailand. At the conclusion of that conflict, nearly 900,000 Vietnamese left northern Vietnam to settle in the south. During the years of Western intervention in Vietnam, nearly 40 percent of the country's rural population moved to avoid the fighting. In the final communist offensive of 1975, hundreds of thousands of Vietnamese became refugees.

Between 1975 and 1978, over 150,000 persons fled Pol Pot's brutality in Cambodia by crossing into Vietnam, while 140,000 left Laos and

Cambodia for Thailand in the same period. Five successive waves of boat people fled Vietnam. The first, totaling 130,000, left with U.S. forces in April–May 1975. The second lasted for three years (until May 1978) and involved the relatively small number of 30,000. The third (June–December 1978) was a product of deteriorating Sino-Vietnamese relations. Some 200,000 ethnic Chinese went overland into the PRC, while 60,000 fled by boat to the ASEAN countries and Hong Kong. The fourth wave followed the Chinese invasion of Vietnam (March–July 1979) when another 175,000 boat people landed on the shores of Malaysia, Indonesia, Hong Kong, and the Philippines. Wave five began in July 1979 when the SRV, responding to international pressures, agreed to control the exodus. Since that time, the outflow of refugees has been comparable to 1975–1978 levels. The rampant bribery through which the refugees obtained the right to leave Vietnam during the third and fourth waves provided the rationale for ASEAN treatment of the boat people as illegal immigrants, fleeing primarily for economic reasons.

While the boat people have been predominantly ethnic Chinese and seek permanent homes outside Vietnam to re-establish their lives, the thousands of Khmer refugees who crossed the land boundary into eastern Thailand present a very different and much more politically volatile problem. With the Vietnamese occupation of Cambodia and the establishment of almost 200,000 VPA forces there, the existence of a variety of anti-Vietnamese and anticommunist resistance movements, with a total membership of several tens of thousands, along the Thai frontier became incendiary. Initially, Thai military and border officials tried to separate the refugees into pro–Pol Pot, anticommunist, and apolitical categories. But by mid-1979, the overwhelming influx made this impossible.

By housing anti-SRV refugees near the border, Thailand had become a virtual belligerent in both the Vietnam-Cambodia war and indirectly in the Sino-Vietnam conflict as well. While publicly abjuring such a role, Thailand, in fact, had decided to facilitate China's assistance to the Pol Pot guerrillas and has permitted small Khmer resistance units to cross into Thailand, move along the Thai side of the border in search of safer terrain, and then re-enter Cambodia.[39]

There are several explanations for this provocative refugee policy. Fundamental is Bangkok's insistence that Thailand will not become a new home for hardened killers (Pol Pot's forces) or a long-term sanctuary for forces bent on overthrowing a neighboring government (the Palestinian parallel). Thai officials also fear the possibility of an eventual linkup between the Khmer Rouge and Thai communist insurgents since China supports both. Most important of all is the fear that the refugees

MAP 1

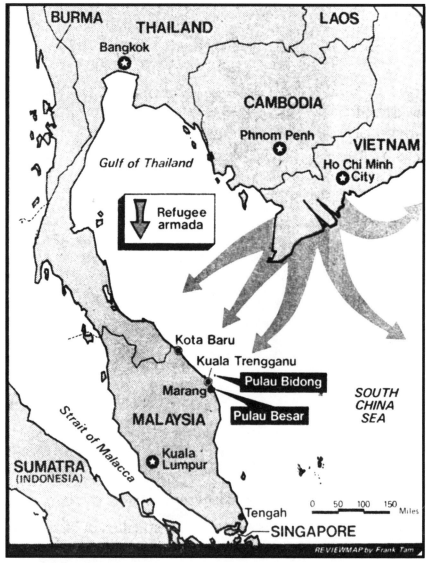

SOURCE: *Far Eastern Economic Review*, December 22, 1978, p. 9.

will bring the war to Thailand either by providing an excuse for an expansionist Vietman or by provoking a "defensive" reaction from Indochina to protect puppet regimes in Laos and Cambodia from dissidents
who fled to Thailand.

No policy could be fully satisfactory. If Thailand welcomes the refugees as urged by the international community in the wake of Vietnam's
invasion of Cambodia, the border regions where refugee camps are located become recruiting areas for anti-Vietnamese movements and
hence targets for artillery attacks and cross-border raids of the kind that
occurred in June 1980. If Bangkok encourages and assists the refugees to
return to Cambodia, it is open to accusations of helping Pol Pot re-
plenish Khmer Rouge forces since much of the border region is under
the latter's control.

Moreover, Thailand's cooperation in the U.N.-sponsored food distribution program across the Cambodian border has attracted up to a
half million people from central and western Cambodia desperately in
need of rice. They remain, for the most part, on the Cambodian side of
the border but could cross over if military and economic conditions deteriorate further. Both the Hanoi and Phnom Penh regimes bitterly opposed the food distribution from the West as a disguised subsidy for the
Khmer Rouge and gross interference in the Democratic Republic of
Kampuchea's internal affairs. By 1981, the food situation in Cambodia
had improved greatly as a result of massive assistance from the Soviet
bloc to Phnom Penh and the U.N. and Western relief agencies along
the Thai-Cambodian border. Nevertheless, droughts and floods in late
1981 portend another food crisis for 1982. International relief efforts will
remain a political issue.

On balance, Thai officials have concluded that the "least worst" policy is to return the refugees to Cambodia whenever possible. Should
Vietnam succeed in sealing the Thai-Cambodian border, several hundred thousand refugees would, in effect, be isolated in Thailand, unable
to return without Hanoi's permission. At the same time, a prolonged
absence of the Cambodians could spur Hanoi to colonize this important
rice bowl with Vietnamese settlers, thus creating a "greater Vietnam"
on Thailand's border. Meanwhile, the presence of squalid refugee
camps consisting of hundreds of thousands of Khmers condemned to
indefinite exile would certainly create serious internal strains for Thailand.[40] Indeed, as part of its warning to Thailand about the latter's vulnerability to refugee moves, Vietnam's raid in June 1980 drove an
estimated 100,000 Cambodians across the border, bringing the total
number of refugees since the January 1979 SRV invasion to approximately 300,000.[41]

Malaysia, the other ASEAN country most affected by the refugee exodus, expresses a somewhat different concern. It believes that Hanoi's apparent decision to expel ethnic Chinese from Cambodia as well as Vietnam was not only a means of ridding itself of a perceived internal fifth column but also a way of destabilizing ASEAN by upsetting the social balance in countries such as Malaysia. The growing anti-Chinese sentiment within ASEAN would be projected toward the PRC, serving Hanoi's goal of undermining ASEAN-China relations.[42] As of the summer of 1979, however, Malaysia's chief psychological warfare official, C. C. Too, could find no evidence that any of the ethnic Chinese refugees were a source of new personnel for the MCP, which remains primarily a village-based organization.[43]

The Sino-Soviet Dimension

An important component of the Vietnamese challenge to ASEAN is the Sino-Soviet dispute. Rivalry within Southeast Asia between the two great communist states accelerated after the American withdrawal from Indochina in 1975. Beijing warned the countries of the region not to let "the [Soviet] tiger in the back door while driving the [U.S.] wolf out the front." For its part, Moscow warned against Chinese efforts to capture Southeast Asian markets by using its oil to secure economic footholds in Thailand and the Philippines.

Moscow found a more profitable issue in China's support of insurgent movements in the region and their possible linkage to Overseas Chinese communities in a number of Southeast Asian countries. Several area governments have been uneasy about the PRC's distinction between party-to-party and government-to-government relations. (This rationalizes the Chinese party's direction of communist insurgencies while the Beijing government maintains ostensibly cordial relations with the governments of those states in which the insurgencies are located.) China is in a delicate position with respect to these movements. On the one hand it has to render enough support to the rebels so that they will not opt for Moscow and Hanoi, and on the other it must assure the governments of the region that China will not interfere in their efforts to quell domestic rebellions.

Up to a point, Sino-Soviet competition was a salutary development in Southeast Asia. By refusing to take sides, the ASEAN states further underscored their commitment to nonalignment. Also, some economic benefits did accrue from China's willingness to sell petroleum products at a "friendship price." Indeed, China's decision to normalize state-to-state relations after 1975 and de-emphasize regional insurgencies as an important foreign policy tool may be attributed to Russian competition in the region.

While the ASEAN states disagree over China's long-term intentions and capabilities, as long as Indochina also remained uncommitted in the Sino-Soviet rivalry, ASEAN had more room to maneuver in its dealings with communist states. This began to change in 1978 when the PRC urged that ASEAN become part of a "joint front" against the USSR. Then, in rapid succession, the Vietnamese-Soviet alliance, Hanoi's invasion of Cambodia, and China's limited military response radically altered the impact of the Sino-Soviet dispute on ASEAN. As Thailand became a front-line state directly threatened by Vietnam, China actively exploited the situation by pointing out that its military confrontation with Vietnam in support of the Khmer Rouge guerrillas directly benefited Bangkok and indirectly protected ASEAN as a whole. In short, ASEAN should join China in a united front against Soviet-Vietnamese expansionism.

Beijing's appeal has been more effective with some ASEAN members than others, creating a certain degree of diplomatic stress within the Association. Although no ASEAN member, including Thailand, has explicitly endorsed China's offer to become a Thai protector, Bangkok clearly welcomes the PRC's belligerence toward Vietnam since it forces Hanoi to station VPA forces along its northern border, relieving some of the pressure along the Thai-Cambodian frontier. China's policy is also welcome in Singapore and, to a degree, the Philippines. Malaysia and Indonesia assess it much less enthusiastically; there the fear of increasing PRC prominence in Southeast Asian matters reinforces fears over the fifth-column potential of the local Chinese population in both countries. Indonesian military leaders still recall China's involvement in the abortive 1965 coup and refuse to establish diplomatic relations. Moreover, Jakarta's military leaders view Indonesia's own Chinese population as a potential fifth column should relations with the PRC be normalized. In Malaysia's case, the approximately one-third of the population that is Chinese dominates the major cities and the commercial sector. For Jakarta and Kuala Lumpur, a strong Vietnam possesses considerable appeal over the long term as a counterweight to Chinese influence. If Hanoi seemed content with a hegemonic position in Indochina, at least two ASEAN capitals would be disposed to accept the situation gracefully.[44]

Meanwhile, China has pressed ASEAN to encourage the United States not only to maintain but to augment its regional military pressure through naval and air force buildups. Beijing argues that although a praiseworthy idea, ZOPFAN cannot operate in an environment of increasing Soviet-Vietnamese aggressiveness. Therefore, ASEAN must continue to rely upon U.S. military force to balance and deter the growing Soviet Pacific Fleet with its access to Vietnamese ports. On related issues with strategic implications, the PRC has also associated itself with ASEAN, particularly when the ASEAN stance complicates Soviet interests. Thus, Beijing supports the Malaysian-Indonesian declaration that the Strait of Malacca is a national water, in the hope of rendering it diplomatically more difficult for the USSR to move its military vessels between the Indian Ocean and the South China Sea. (Of course, this position also complicates the passage of the American navy and, in the future, a Chinese blue-water navy as well.)

In global diplomatic affairs after 1974, the PRC advocated the creation of the broadest possible united front, combining all three of Mao's "worlds," against the USSR.[45] By 1979, Beijing's notion of a global united front now included the United States—heretofore a member of the First World of superpowers. Some Southeast Asian countries welcomed the prospect of a tacit alliance between the PRC and the United States, believing it would offset growing Soviet activity and contribute to regional stability.[46]

The Vietnamese invasion of Cambodia and the subsequent Chinese incursion, however, dashed these hopes for regional peace.[47] In an address to the U.N. Security Council, the Chinese representative warned that the Soviet Union was using Vietnam to create an enclave on the Asian mainland from which "to control the sea-lane from the west Pacific to the Indian Ocean and link up its strategic deployments in the two oceans so as to prepare for the seizure of oil resources and important strategic positions in west Asia and the Middle East."[48]

PRC pundits pictured the USSR as moving to position itself to cut off European and Japanese energy resources by controlling the sea-lanes between the Persian Gulf and East Asia. Afghanistan and Indochina were two parts of an envelopment strategy and not just isolated incidents divorced from Moscow's long-term goals:

If the Soviet Union continues to advance westward into Iran and the Arabian Peninsula, and eastward into South Asia, while Vietnam expands from Indochina into Southeast Asia, then they will form a pincer against the Malacca Strait, the sea route between the two oceans. They can also threaten the Makassar Strait and the Lombok Strait. Once such a move is completed, the Soviet Union will be in a position to control the supply lines of raw materials and energy as well as the trade routes of Japan, Western Europe and the Asian and African countries. Soviet control of the Middle East, Persian Gulf, Southeast Asia and the Malacca

Strait would mean the completion in the main of the Soviet global strategic deployment for world domination. Therefore, one must consider the Soviet aggression against Afghanistan and Vietnam's aggression against Kampuchea from strategic perspectives and take a long-term view instead of seeing them as isolated and regional events.[49]

American military involvement in Southeast Asia will inevitably benefit the PRC. American political and military commitments to countries such as Thailand may deter the USSR from further military involvement or at least limit the amount of support it is willing to provide Vietnam. A Soviet withdrawal would weaken the USSR's credibility as an ally and reduce its influence in the SRV, making it necessary for Vietnam to seek a modus vivendi with Beijing. On the other hand, a Soviet challenge to the United States and ASEAN would poison Soviet-American relations further and weaken détente. Either way, China gains.

China also claims to support ASEAN hopes for regional neutralization, although Beijing is skeptical of the chances for its realization. The PRC's invasion of Vietnam, from this point of view, was a demonstration of its willingness to serve as guarantor to Thailand. By engaging in a courageous and dangerous indirect confrontation with the USSR in Vietnam, China, in effect, proved its good intentions toward ASEAN and contributed to the latter's regional neutralization policy. Indeed, China is the only major actor to have challenged the Vietnam-Soviet alliance. Reinforcing this position, the PRC reportedly pledged support for the Philippines if its security were threatened.[50]

ASEAN has come closest to a breach in its united opposition to Vietnam's occupation of Cambodia over the issue of Soviet versus Chinese influence in Southeast Asia. Meeting at the Malaysian coastal city of Kuantan, Malaysian Prime Minister Hussein Onn and Indonesian President Suharto agreed that a solution to the Cambodian problem must be based on the principle that Vietnam remain outside both the Soviet and the Chinese spheres of influence. Implicit in this declaration was the possibility of accepting Vietnam's hegemony in Indochina, including the presence of Hanoi's forces in Cambodia, if the SRV somehow cut its ties with the Soviet Union.[51]

The so-called Kuantan declaration created a serious diplomatic problem for ASEAN. Singapore dissociated itself almost immediately as Foreign Minister Rajaratnam warned that Soviet expansionism through Vietnam's Cambodian adventure could force ASEAN to abandon nonalignment and turn to other great powers for protection. In effect, Singapore was repeating the PRC's strategic assessment of Soviet intentions.[52] Thailand concurred with the Kuantan declaration's purpose of weaning Vietnam away from the USSR but could not endorse the pres-

ence of Vietnamese forces in Cambodia. To do so would be to repudi-
ate ASEAN's November 1979 U.N. General Assembly resolution
calling for a complete Vietnamese withdrawal.

While rejecting the anti-Soviet implications of the Kuantan declaration, the SRV has proffered at least one carrot for ASEAN recognition
of the Heng Samrin regime in Cambodia. In exchange for ASEAN's
recognition of the People's Republic of Kampuchea, Hanoi would recognize ASEAN as an international body with which negotiations could
be conducted.[53]

ASEAN confronts a series of complicated political calculations with
respect to the Sino-Soviet conflict in Indochina. One line of argument,
espoused by Malaysia, Indonesia, and some elements in the U.S. State
Department, holds that acceptance of a broadened version of the current Heng Samrin regime in Cambodia will reduce regional tension and
diminish both Soviet and Chinese influence in Southeast Asia as the
search for outside allies declines. Behind this approach is the premise
that Vietnam's ambitions are limited to Indochina and that Hanoi desires both to reduce its almost total dependence on the USSR and to
ameliorate relations with China. The opposite view, held most strongly
by Thailand, Singapore, and the Philippines, is that Hanoi will even-
tually compromise if international political pressure is maintained
through the United Nations, if anti-Vietnamese forces are supplied and
given sanctuary along the Thai border, if economic aid is denied to
Vietnam, and if the threat of a second Chinese attack is sustained. This
line of argument is premised on a tacit Sino-U.S. alliance and opposition
to accommodation with Hanoi. Should the United States decide to
reach a modus vivendi with the SRV on its own, American and Chinese policies toward the region would diverge. This would place Thailand in a particularly awkward position, forcing it to choose between its
two major outside supporters against the Soviet-Vietnam threat.

Time may well be on the side of Moscow and Hanoi. If the Russians
are willing to sustain a spending level of over $6 million per day for
Indochina, ultimately there would seem to be little alternative to accepting some variant of the current Cambodian regime in a colonial relationship to Vietnam. The Khmer Rouge is not an acceptable alternative to
either international opinion or the Khmer population; and the noncommunist resistance movement is virtually anarchic, despite efforts in 1981
to create a united front. An Indochinese federation under Hanoi's control need not threaten Thailand (providing some arrangements were de-
vised for the approximately 500,000 Cambodians on both sides of the
Thai-Cambodian border) and could be a factor for regional stability insofar as it balanced Chinese ambitions.

Meanwhile, ASEAN is imbedded in the middle of one more side of the multifaceted Sino-Soviet dispute. China has openly declared it wants to see Hanoi bled white in Indochina. Its position is totally uncompromising, and it has urged ASEAN and the United States to adopt a similar stance. The Soviet Union is not displeased with China's intransigence since it keeps Hanoi committed to Moscow, adding a Southeast Asian dimension to an apparent Soviet policy of expanding military influence in Third World regions astride major trade routes. Malaysia and Indonesia believe the Kuantan principle offers Hanoi a way out of this dilemma at a cost to Hanoi of a virtual tradeoff—the breaking of its treaty with the USSR in exchange for recognition of its pre-eminence in Indochina. But Kuala Lumpur and Jakarta have been unable to convince either their ASEAN partners or China that such a course would really affect the Soviet-Vietnam relationship or reduce regional tension.

The Sino-Vietnamese Dimension

The most dangerous aspect of the Sino-Soviet conflict in Southeast Asia is the Sino-Vietnamese confrontation. Once Vietnam opted for the USSR in 1978, military movements by either the PRC or SRV involved the USSR almost immediately as arms supplier to Hanoi. Hanoi's apparent ability to tap Soviet supplies at will severely limits ASEAN's ability to negotiate a lower level of confrontation over the SRV's control of Cambodia and threat to Thailand. In short, ASEAN can offer Vietnam virtually nothing compared to what it can obtain through Soviet largesse.

This is not to say that Vietnam is uninterested in improving relations with ASEAN. Hanoi indicated a desire to do so in early 1978 when it dropped its earlier insistence that the Association was merely an extension of such U.S.-dominated military alliances as SEATO. Visits by high-level Vietnamese officials to ASEAN capitals beginning in late 1977 led to statements that the time was ripe to improve relations. By normalizing relations with Thailand and seeking trade agreements, Vietnam demonstrated its desire for bilateral conciliation with its neighbors. By putting forth its own idea for a region of "peace, independence, freedom, and neutrality," Hanoi signaled its interest in ordering Southeast Asian relations both within the region and with outside forces. Trade agreements signed in 1978 with Thailand and Malaysia granting most-favored-nation status and payment in local currency showed that Vietnam could benefit from regional trade and technical cooperation agreements. Malaysia offered to make its expertise available to assist in the rehabilitation of Vietnam's war-damaged rubber plantations. Thailand wanted an agreement allowing Thai fishing in Vietnamese waters for a share of the profits, and Singapore could offer investment and expertise in consumer industries.

China had backed ASEAN much earlier than Vietnam did.[54] By 1973, the PRC became interested in seeing that the Association was not attached to the Soviet Asian collective security proposal. Beijing thus supported ZOPFAN, for a zone of neutrality would preclude a Soviet military presence and forestall any Vietnamese-Russian alliance. China's strong support for Thailand, particularly after Vietnam's victories in 1975, revealed the emergence of a new lineup in the region—Pol Pot's Cambodia, Thailand, and the PRC against Vietnam and Laos— that could block Hanoi's ambitions in Indochina. If Vietnam succeeded in dominating Indochina without resistance from Beijing, the latter would find its influence waning throughout the region. But Chinese resistance to Hanoi's ambitions, although helpful to ASEAN, would provide the Soviets an opening into regional politics on Vietnam's side. This is precisely what happened during 1978; Hanoi first joined COMECON and then signed a quasi-military alliance with the USSR. The agreements served to replace Chinese aid and deter any counterattack by China's army as Vietnam prepared to invade Cambodia.

Vietnam attempted to preclude any effective Chinese response to its initiatives. In visits to ASEAN leaders in the fall of 1978, Vietnam's prime minister and foreign minister both promised that the SRV would neither support insurgent movements within ASEAN nor threaten the territorial integrity of its members. In retrospect, Hanoi probably believed that these visits would reassure the ASEAN states, once they learned of Vietnam's invasion of Cambodia, that its ambitions did not extend beyond Indochina. Moreover, by portraying the ethnic Chinese in Vietnam as a fifth column, Hanoi probably hoped to stimulate the anti-Chinese feelings lurking just beneath the surface in several of the ASEAN states. If China did react militarily to Vietnam's depredations, then Hanoi could argue that the PRC would similarly challenge other Southeast Asian states attempting to cope with their own perfidious Chinese. In sum, Vietnam appeared to calculate that ASEAN would welcome both its efforts to force an exodus of its ethnic Chinese and its invasion of Cambodia since these acts would enhance the SRV's ability to block China's ambitions in Southeast Asia through subversion of the Overseas Chinese. Hanoi thought it was teaching the rest of the region how to deal with China. To a certain extent, its calculations were not entirely misplaced. Indonesian elites, for example, were not adverse to a Hanoi-led Indochina for exactly these reasons.[55]

Beijing was aware of the awkward position into which Hanoi was attempting to maneuver it with respect to the Overseas Chinese community. The PRC felt an obligation to Chinese singled out for discrimination in other countries, but at the same time it wished to reassure these countries that their Chinese citizens would abide by local laws and customs and not serve as a fifth column. With Vietnam in mind, Chinese Central Committee member Liao Zhengzhi wrote:

> Upon acquiring the nationality of their country of residence, the Overseas Chinese became citizens of that country and lose their Chinese nationality automatically. *We do not recognize dual nationality, but we regard it as impermissible to compel Overseas Chinese to choose one nationality or another. Those who have chosen the nationality of their country of residence are still our kinfolk even though they are no longer Chinese citizens.* [Emphasis added.] We require that Overseas Chinese abide by the law of their countries of residence, respect the customs and habits of the people of these countries, learn the languages of these countries and play an active role in developing the economy and culture of these countries. . . . We require that Overseas Chinese guard against the ideas of great nation chauvinism. . . . We also hope that the countries where Overseas Chinese live will respect their legitimate rights and interests and their national tradition, customs, and habits.[56]

Beijing was holding out both a carrot and stick to those countries with significant numbers of Overseas Chinese. If reasonably treated, these people would make a major contribution to the commercial development of their adopted countries—with the PRC's blessing. If they were subjected to persecution, however, China would not disavow them and might come to their assistance. Beijing's statement aroused little concern in such states as Thailand—the Sino-Thai were well integrated and established in Thai capitalism. The Overseas Chinese were no obstacle to cordial PRC-Thai relations, then, when Vietnam invaded Cambodia and refugees from a variety of ethnic communities crossed the Thai border.

As the VPA geared up to march into Cambodia behind the fig leaf of a "liberation front," Beijing warned:

> It is noteworthy that Vo Nguyen Giap stressed the need for all Vietnamese officers and men to recognize the "new targets of war." What did he mean, besides China and Kampuchea, when he talked of the "new targets of war" and "international reactionary forces"? This cannot but arouse the vigilance of the Southeast Asian countries. After the creation of a puppet Kampuchean organization by the Vietnamese authorities, Singapore Foreign Minister Rajaratnam said: "The Vietnamese have set up a Cambodian national salvation front. We are concerned whether two years from now it would be necessary to set up salvation

fronts for ASEAN countries. What is happening in Kampuchea today could happen to us tomorrow."[57]

As the Vietnamese marched into Cambodia, China quickly moved to associate itself with ASEAN in opposition. Within days after the invasion, the PRC signed a five-year contract with Thailand stipulating the supply of approximately one million tons of crude oil per year through 1983. Prices would be negotiated annually, taking into account the "friendly" relations between the two countries.[58] China also began a resupply of Pol Pot's forces both across Thailand and through islands off the Thai-Cambodian coastline.

Other ASEAN states—particularly Indonesia and Malaysia—remained skeptical of China's benevolent intentions. President Suharto mentioned that the PRC continued to provide sanctuary for Indonesian Communist Party (PKI) leaders and that China had stated it would not sever party-to-party links with insurgent movements in the region. Despite Hanoi's invasion of Cambodia, Suharto displayed little apprehension over the prospect of Vietnamese forces advancing beyond Indochina. He took heart at Pham Van Dong's assurances that Hanoi would not support communist movements in other Southeast Asian countries.[59] The SRV underscored this theme by insisting that any threat to ASEAN came from China's ambitions for regional domination, not Hanoi's. Warning ASEAN not to cooperate with Beijing, Vietnamese pundits asked rhetorically: "What would be the fate of the countries in the region if the Indochina bastion should ever unfortunately collapse? They fail to understand this: Beijing's tools would immediately begin their work and the publicly known fifth columnists would not hesitate to brandish their swords and behead all those who might oppose them."[60]

Nevertheless, ASEAN presented a resolution at the U.N. Security Council calling for "foreign forces" to withdraw from Vietnam and Cambodia. China's compliance with the resolution served to emphasize its underlying common interests with ASEAN and made Beijing appear the more accommodating of the two antagonistic Asian communist states. Beijing was further delighted as Vietnam's intransigence over any kind of troop withdrawal pushed ASEAN inevitably (if reluctantly) toward China. As VPA forces deployed along the Thai border and engaged in skirmishes, some of which spilled over from time to time, the PRC warned that ASEAN's security was now threatened directly.[61]

Deng Xiaoping pledged China's support for ASEAN efforts against the Vietnam threat and urged the Association to "play a greater part in safeguarding peace in ... Southeast Asia."[62] Chinese officials rationalized the PRC's aid to the Khmer Rouge as a way of blocking the Vietnamese from expanding the war into Thailand and Malaysia.[63] Finally, Deng told a visiting Thai deputy premier that Beijing would come to Bangkok's rescue "in every way" if Thailand's security were threatened.[64]

Noteworthy, too, was the condemnation of Vietnam by the pro-Beijing Communist Party of Thailand (CPT) and its implied promise to fight with the government should the SRV attempt to carry the war into Thailand. Moreover, the CPT was concerned that Hanoi would try to set up its own version of the party with defectors who remained in Laos after the VPA and Laotian army forced the Thai Communists out of their accustomed sanctuary along the Lao-Thai border.[65]

Thai analysts point out that their country had come to a modus vivendi with the Pol Pot regime by 1977, after which border fighting between the two countries diminished. This was in line with the belief that the real threat to Thailand derived not from Beijing's rhetorical support for the CPT but rather from Hanoi's desire to control Indochina. An independent Cambodia—even under the Khmer Rouge—posed no real danger to Thailand; but that same country as part of a Vietnamese bloc would be a formidable threat and require that Thailand develop outside support against it. That support could come from Washington, Beijing, or even ASEAN—although the last is seen as least likely to provide anything significant.[66]

By the fall of 1979, the SRV began to take a harder line toward ASEAN, viewing it as part of an anti–Soviet/Vietnamese axis that included Washington-Beijing-Tokyo-Seoul. Hanoi openly accused Thailand of becoming a "hideout" for Pol Pot's forces, "who receive help from the Thai authorities in the form of transportation of . . . supplies, food, weapons, and medical treatment. Certain areas of Thailand have become a beachhead for the Pol Pot remnant troops to launch offensives into Kampuchea" with weapons provided by Beijing.[67]

Vietnamese officials also argued that for the time being there was no *practical* alternative to VPA forces in Cambodia. Should they withdraw, not only would anarchy prevail because of the resulting political vacuum, but the return of Pol Pot's entourage would lead to a new bloodbath. Moreover, a VPA withdrawal would destroy the relief conduit to the Cambodian people, leaving them to starve.[68]

By 1980, the SRV had established a rationale for the indefinite occupation of Cambodia. Foreign Minister Nguyen Co Thach stated that although the VPA could eliminate the Khmer Rouge, it has refrained from violating Pol Pot's sanctuaries in Thailand in order to maintain good relations with the Bangkok government. Nevertheless, Thach insisted that Vietnamese forces would stay in Cambodia not only until the Khmer Rouge threat was eliminated but also while a threat from China existed, presumably both to the SRV's northern border and to Laos.[69] In effect, Hanoi was pressuring Thailand to help persuade the PRC to reduce its military challenge to Vietnam. VPA General Von Tien Dung summarized Hanoi's view of the situation:

> As long as Beijing, which is in complicity with imperialism and other reactionary forces, threatens the independence and sovereignty of our three countries, the presence of the Vietnamese Army in the two fraternal countries will be necessary. When the threat of interference, subversive activity and aggression from outside ceases to exist, then the need for the Vietnamese Army's presence in Laos and Kampuchea will also disappear. This is the common position of the three fraternal states.[70]

Singapore's Deputy Prime Minister Sinnathamby Rajaratnam interpreted Vietnam's new condition for withdrawal from Cambodia as a linking of the Sino-Vietnamese and the Sino-Soviet conflicts.[71] Because Vietnam depended on Russian aid to sustain its occupation of Laos and Cambodia, Moscow may well have stipulated that continuation of that support would depend on a persistent Vietnamese threat to China's southern border regions, forcing the PRC both to split its military deployment and to divert resources away from industrial and agricultural modernization. SRV Foreign Minister Thach advised ASEAN that if it wanted to see stability restored in Southeast Asia, it should stop demanding the withdrawal of Vietnamese troops and instead "put pressure on China to remove its threat."[72]

Vietnam has been trying to encourage differences between ASEAN and China over Cambodia. While Beijing seeks to eliminate Vietnam as a major actor in Southeast Asia— "to bleed it white" —ASEAN wishes only to see Cambodia's autonomy restored. ASEAN would not wish to see a pro-Beijing Khmer Rouge government brought back to power even if that were feasible. Such a government, aligned to the PRC, would be equally destabilizing to the region, for it would be unacceptable to both Hanoi and Moscow. The price for Soviet and Vietnamese acceptance of an independent Cambodia may well be a government that leans toward Hanoi diplomatically but does not require the presence of VPA troops to keep it in power. ASEAN would probably be willing to live with such a regime, for over time it could also be part of a protective barrier against any expansionist ambitions by a newly modernized China. Despite the congruence of certain long-term interests of ASEAN and Vietnam, however, the Association remains united in its opposition to political change brought about by outside aggression. The vulnerability of many ASEAN members to the same kind of assault makes them unwilling to accept Vietnam's fait accompli with equanimity.

Moreover, China offers no real solution to the Cambodian issue. PRC Foreign Minister Huang Hua has stated that the struggle to get the Vietnamese out of Cambodia will be long and arduous. Only when Hanoi and Moscow find it too costly to maintain their aggression will they seek a political solution.[73] There is no indication, however, that either side had reached that point by 1981.

China has tried to move Thailand away from its official position of neutrality in the Sino-Vietnamese dispute. In a winter 1980 visit to Bangkok, National People's Congress Vice-Chairman Deng Yingchao stated that since Thailand recognized Democratic Kampuchea, there was no point in remaining neutral in the conflict. China's effusive promises of aid to Thailand in the event of an attack also appear designed to align that country with the PRC.[74] Beijing may reason that if Thailand were to commit itself to the PRC, ASEAN would have to condone the decision since Thailand was the threatened, front-line member. Indeed, a primary reason for the Indonesian-Malaysian meeting at Kuantan was to preempt a Thai alignment with China by urging that Vietnam itself accept a nonaligned position vis-à-vis the USSR and China in exchange for ASEAN's acceptance of its hegemonial role in Indochina and the Heng Samrin regime in Cambodia. Hanoi's rejection of the Kuantan principle probably stemmed from its deep dependence on the USSR and its belief that China would be unwilling to accept Vietnam's position in the region even if ASEAN would. Hanoi sees the Association's proposal of U.N.-supervised elections and the disarmament of all Khmer factions as both infeasible and likely to restore an anti-Vietnamese regime dependent for its survival on China and the United States. The Vietnamese argue that Cambodian neutrality terminated with Sihanouk's ouster in 1970. Even the fragile nonalignment maintained by the prince between 1955 and 1970 required an alliance between China and Vietnam. The reversion of those two states to their traditional posture of hostility precludes an independent, nonaligned Cambodia. The country will be responsive either to the PRC or the SRV, and Hanoi sees no reason to abandon its Cambodian allies so that its adversaries can gain control.[75]

ASEAN's efforts to tread the line between Vietnam and China were severely tested in June 1980, when, after the Thais had begun to repatriate several thousand Cambodians into Khmer Rouge–held territory, VPA forces temporarily crossed the Thai border. ASEAN members rallied behind Bangkok, uniformly condemning Hanoi. Vietnam's behavior once again tarnished its reputation as a liberator of oppressed peoples. It was acting instead as a regional hegemonist, employing its military might to dominate weaker neighbors. The payoff is control over one of Southeast Asia's richest rice bowls and possibly even Thailand, the world's largest rice exporter in 1979. (The SRV by contrast had to import 1.3 million tons in 1979 and was over 4 million tons short in 1980.) Put another way, Vietman has 51 million people who are short of rice while Cambodia has 4.5 million in one of Asia's most fertile regions. As Bangkok's *Nation Review* editorialized on June 24:

> Oh yes, Hanoi must know that nobody in Bangkok or along the eastern border is stupid. Everyone knows that what the Vietnamese want is to halt the repatriation of the refugees.
>
> But from Hanoi's point of view: Thailand is damned if it does and it is damned if it doesn't. When for humanitarian reasons, Thailand took about 200,000 refugees, this country was blamed for harboring Khmer Rouge guerrillas. When the refugees want to go back to their home-land—their homeland, to repeat—and are supervised by international agencies, then Thailand is accused of helping the Khmer Rouge guer-rillas. What sort of a people are those who want to kill refugees in camps while the international community is stretching itself to feed them and give medical attention?

Vietnam confronts a dilemma. It is unwilling to surrender control of Indochina; yet it cannot have peace with China unless it does so. In order to maintain its hegemonic position, Hanoi must rely on the USSR—an alliance that reinforces China's intransigence. As long as Vietnamese troops occupy Cambodia, ASEAN will see them as threat-ening to Thailand. This situation has created parallel interests between the PRC and the noncommunist Southeast Asian group.

Vietnam's state of war in Cambodia, its occupation of Laos, and its near war with China are destroying its economy. This, in turn, increases its dependence on the USSR. China is not really unhappy about these developments, despite its rhetoric. It costs Beijing little to sustain re-sistance in Cambodia, particularly since the 500,000 refugees along the Thai-Cambodian border form a potential Palestinian-type resistance. Vietnam's continued economic malaise may well increase draconian ec-onomic measures at home, leading to further refugee flight and hence further exacerbation of its relations with the ASEAN countries.

The SRV's dominance in Indochina is humiliating to Beijing. Just as Chinese forces pose a second-front threat to Vietman on behalf of Thai-land, so Soviet troops perform the same function for the SRV vis-à-vis China. Moreover, Hanoi's conquest of Indochina demonstrates China's military and political weakness—its inability to control political change on its own borders. Not only did this reveal that China is not a global power, but it also called into question whether it was much of a regional actor as well.

Another factor plays a role in the Sino-Vietnamese conflict and its challenge to ASEAN: maritime boundary disputes. Vietnam claims that in 1974, the two countries agreed to defer oil prospecting in a 20,000 square kilometer zone in the Gulf of Tonkin midway between Hainan Island and the Vietnam coast pending negotiations to determine the sea frontier. But, in 1979, as relations between the two states crumbled, China unilaterally signed a contract with a U.S. oil consortium to initiate seismic soundings. Hanoi vehemently protested this action. It feared that acceptance of the consortium's activities could be construed as recognition of China's interpretation of the disputed boundary. This, in turn, had strategic implications, for the PRC could blockade the port of Haiphong by forces deployed from Hainan and the Paracels. Beijing has recognized its vulnerability off the Paracels, and it is probably no coincidence that all exploration in the disputed area is being conducted by American consortia, evidently in the hope that the potential involvement of the U.S. Navy might deter a Vietnamese or Soviet challenge.

China's sea boundary claims in the South China Sea are grossly exaggerated (see Maps 2 and 3) and cover virtually the entire basin to within twenty miles of Kalimantan, leading to disputes with Indonesia, Malaysia, and the Philippines, as well as with Vietnam. The most serious are with the Philippines and Vietnam. Over Chinese protests, the Philippines occupied the island of Thitu, and a U.S.-Swedish-Filipino consortium initiated drilling off the nearby Reed Bank. In Vietnam's case the potential for confrontation is high since Hanoi controls the Spratlys in the southwest while Beijing has occupied the Paracels since January 1974. These island groupings are particularly important as strategic locations astride trade routes from the South China Sea into the Malacca Strait and Indian Ocean.

In September 1979, at about the same time that Beijing signed oil exploration contracts with American companies, it announced four "danger zones" around Hainan Island, warning foreign airlines against uncleared overflights. Hanoi denounced the flight ban as the next step in China's progressive efforts to annex the South China Sea.[76]

In contrast to the PRC's intransigence over maritime claims, Hanoi has been somewhat more flexible on these matters, at least with ASEAN states. Thus, the SRV conveyed its willingness to discuss its dispute with Malaysia over the continental shelf between the two countries off Sabah involving the Spratly Islands. These differences involve

MAP 2
SOUTH CHINA SEA

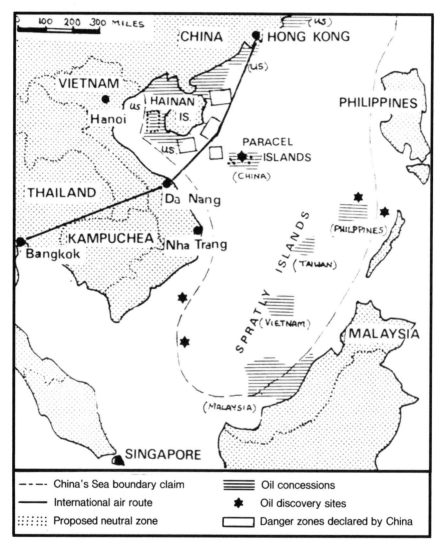

SOURCE: *Vietnam Today* (Bulletin of the Australia Vietnam Society), no. 11 (October–December 1979): 3.

MAP 3
SMALL CHINA SEA: AREAS OF CONFLICT

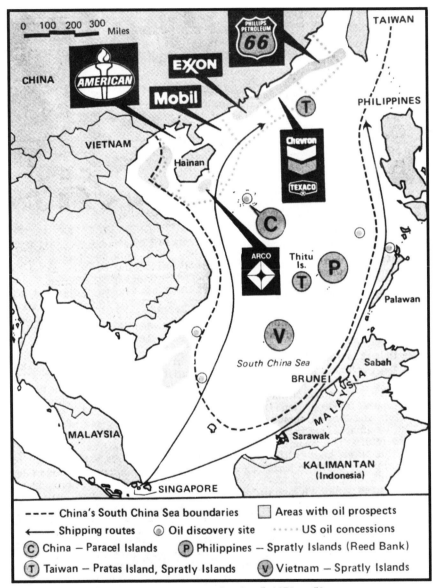

SOURCE: *Far Eastern Economic Review*, October 5, 1979, p. 58.

the disputed Spratly Islands. A separate controversy arises over the Kelantan coast off northeast Malaya, to which claims have been made by Malaysia, Thailand, and Vietnam. Once again, Vietnam has offered to negotiate.[77]

Unless these disputes are amicably resolved through diplomacy before significant resource exploitation begins, they could become military flash points, especially since China is increasing its naval capacity and the USSR is undertaking a greater maritime military role, perhaps on Vietnam's behalf. Given the growing economic stakes inherent in resource exploitation, maritime boundary disputes are political time bombs, awaiting the development by the states involved of a capability to enforce their claims.

Internal Challenges

Besides the threats to ASEAN inherent in hostile alliances involving external powers and in the disputes among China, Vietnam, and the USSR, there are problems endemic to ASEAN that could be exploited by outsiders. The most serious is internal political dissidence arising from ethnic or ideological insurgencies. Of the five member-states, only Singapore does not have a serious domestic insurgency or a divisive ethnic problem. Moreover its wealth is distributed equally, eliminating the threat of conflict between haves and have-nots.

External Aid to Domestic Insurgencies

Much of Thailand's apprehension over Vietnam's domination of Indochina revolves around the possibility of irredentism in some sixteen northeastern Thai provinces where the majority of the population is Lao. The area has also long been a base for guerrilla activities of the CPT. Fortunately for the Thai government, the CPT remains firmly pro-Beijing at a time when Laos has been integrated into the Soviet-Vietnamese camp. This means that earlier training, supply, and sanctuary facilities enjoyed by the CPT in Laos are now denied to it. Additionally debilitating from the CPT's perspective is the reduction in Chinese supplies that followed Beijing's establishment of close relations with Bangkok in 1978. Thus, the CPT challenge in the border areas of the north and northeast is at its lowest level in some years. This is not to deny, however, that a change in the regional political configuration could not lead to a revitalized CPT. Should Chinese relations with Thailand deteriorate, say, over a decision by Bangkok to acquiesce in Hanoi's domination of Cambodia, then China might well revive the CPT as a means of displaying its displeasure. Or, for example, should

Vietnam decide to increase pressure on Bangkok, it could sponsor a new communist movement in northeastern Thailand by reopening the supply lines and sanctuaries in Laos. Nevertheless, by the early 1980s, the CPT's challenge to the central government fell to its lowest level since its inception in 1960. Moreover, in June 1981 the party openly appealed to Bangkok for joint efforts against the Vietnamese occupation of Cambodia.[78]

In the crucial northeastern Isan region of Thailand, the insurgents traditionally drew their principal support from Vietnam through Laos. Between 1976 and 1978, Vietnamese-backed insurgents competed for control of key base areas with their Chinese-backed rivals. Pathet Lao cadres can still move at will through this area and pass themselves off as Thai-Lao.[79] However, as long as the Vietnamese play on irredentist and minority sentiments, their appeal to the majority of Thailand's population will be limited, as the CPT's decision to rally behind the government in the wake of Vietnam's threat to Thai border regions demonstrated. The CPT is undoubtedly aware of the Vietnamese treatment of front groups in neighboring countries that have achieved military victory. The fates of the National Liberation Front in South Vietnam, the Khmer Rouge, and even the Pathet Lao have forewarned CPT cadres about too close an association.

The Vietnamese threat has also served somewhat to neutralize the flight of students from urban Thailand into the jungle after the military crackdown on student demonstrations following the 1976 coup. This had given the CPT a considerable boost as young leaders joined the party in opposition to what was seen as a repressive regime. Although some filtered back to their families over the next few years, many stayed in the jungle. The Vietnamese invasion of Cambodia became something of a turning point in their sentiments, however. A number have either rallied to the government or, while remaining with the party, have pledged to work against the SRV.

Noteworthy here is the discrepancy between rhetoric and behavior. China has refused to renounce its support of regional communist parties. They are too important a source of leverage if official relations with neighbors sour. The cessation of significant Chinese material aid to regional insurgents has, however, reassured the ASEAN governments (with the exception of Indonesia and, to a smaller extent, Malaysia) that in fact the PRC does not pose a threat to domestic order. In contrast, Hanoi has publicly renounced support for communist rebels on several occasions, beginning with Pham Van Dong's September 1978 visit to Association members. Subsequent Vietnamese military thrusts into Cambodia and along the Thai border have undermined the credibility of Hanoi's promises, however. Nor is the Vietnamese ambassador to Indonesia's lame excuse convincing: "What we have done in Kampuchea is not subversion because we are supporting the just struggle of the Kampuchean people."[80] Support for such "just struggles" is precisely what ASEAN leaders believed Pham Van Dong had abjured in his well-publicized trek through the region.

The PRC's lowered profile with respect to regional insurgencies is also apparent in its handling of their periodic statements on party anniversaries and holidays. Messages of congratulations from the Thai, Indonesian, and Malayan parties on China's National Day in October 1979 contained none of the rhetoric of domestic revolution normally found in such statements on previous occasions.[81] By the autumn of 1979, a spokesman for the Thai Border Patrol Police commented that CPT activities in the north and northeast were at their lowest ebb in years.[82] Vietnamese officials hewed to the line that they had no contact with the CPT. Speaking ruefully, Deputy Foreign Minister Phan Hein told a Thai correspondent: "We learned a painful lesson with Pol Pot. Why should we make the same mistake again?"[83]

It is somewhat ironic that with thousands of Khmer refugees arrayed along both sides of the Thai-Cambodian border, it is the Vietnamese Communists and their Cambodian agents who are now most concerned about external aid to subversive forces. For Vietnam and the Heng Samrin regime, the shoe is definitely on the other foot. Instead of fomenting rebellion in a neighboring country, the Vietnamese are trying to suppress a stubborn insurgency within a client's territory—an insurgency provisioned from Beijing and aided by Thailand with the de facto blessing of ASEAN, the United States, and even the U.N. High Commissioner for Rufugees. These are a formidable list of adversaries with which Hanoi must contend, even with the diplomatic and material assistance of the Soviet Union.

Vietnam has accused Thailand of "creating a sanctuary for the remnant Pol Pot army and other reactionary Kampuchean forces so that they can use this as a staging base to sabotage the Kampuchean revolution." Moreover, the SRV has obliquely warned Thailand that it may retaliate: "The incorrect attitude and actions of Thailand will create a danger to you and stability in Thailand."[84]

International relief agencies are generally unable to distinguish between Khmer Rouge fighters and apolitical refugees. All Khmer who appear receive rice and other necessities. Nevertheless, despite the desperate health conditions among those under Khmer Rouge control in 1979–1980, Pol Pot's soldiers may have confiscated much of the rice to feed themselves, leaving the population to fend for itself.[85]

Even Thailand's decision to move large numbers of refugees inland away from the border so that their location would not be so provocative to the Vietnamese is viewed by Hanoi as a maneuver to protect Khmer Rouge forces by giving them time to rest, recuperate, and resupply.[86] Beijing fuels these fears by publicizing Thai links to the Khmer Rouge. Pol Pot, for example, in an interview carried by Beijing Radio, stated that "Thailand and our guerrilla units have trade contacts with each other."[87]

Vietnam also fears the possibility of Chinese-sponsored insurgency in Laos. Northern Laos in particular has been under Chinese influence for years because of the many Chinese military engineers engaged in road building in the area who distributed food and other aid in a region that was generally neglected by the weak Lao government, thus creating goodwill. In late 1979, a shadowy group called the Lao Socialist Party was formed. It is conceivable that the 10,000 Indochinese refugees of Chinese origin taken by China from Thailand may be trained for deployment in northern Laos through neighboring Yunnan province. At least the potential for such action now exists.

Meanwhile, Hanoi may be responding in kind. Despite its promises not to support insurgencies in neighboring countries, reports that a pro-Hanoi Thai communist party was being nurtured among a core of disaffected cadres in Laos appeared in 1980. Known as the Thai Isan Liberation Party and apparently organized in late October 1979 in Vietnam, the organization is led by peasants and workers from northeastern Thailand. The party may be advocating autonomy for the region. If the party becomes popular enough, Hanoi could use it as a bargaining chip to induce Thailand to abandon its ties with the PRC. Chinese leaders indirectly acknowledged the new party's existence when Central Committee member Ji Pengfei spoke of a split in the CPT and actual armed conflict between the two factions.[88]

While the Thai insurgencies in the north and northeast and the Khmer Rouge enclaves along the Thai-Cambodian border constitute the most dangerous challenge to peace in Southeast Asia, other insurgent movements in ASEAN states have received outside assistance. The MCP, operating from the Betong region of south Thailand, has remained impervious to combined Thai-Malaysian efforts to dislodge it. Although external support to this pro-Beijing party is probably not significant, it remains viable by collecting "protection" money in the provincial cities and villages of the south. One Western observer saw these "tax" transactions openly conducted even in the presence of Thai officials, who left the collector unmolested. This same observer believes that fully half of the MCP Politburo lives in southern Thailand, whose ethnic Chinese population has become a major source of recruits. Somewhat over 3,000 guerrillas operate in the border region, although they generally confine their military actions to the Malaysian side. Although there is little evidence to suggest any links between the MCP, Muslim separatists in southern Thailand, and the CPT, the two communist parties have agreed to stay out of each other's territory.[89]

Thai Muslim separatists organized as the Patani United Liberation Organization (PULO) have claimed that Bangkok aids the MCP in order to obtain intelligence on PULO activities. After PULO guerrillas were driven from the MCP stronghold of Betong in March 1981, the former charged that the Thai military had actually supplied the Malayan Communists with arms to help fight the PULO insurgents. The PULO led some 200 Thai Muslim refugees caught in the crossfire to sanctuary on the Malaysian side of the border. This, in turn, fueled Thai intelligence suspicions that the Malaysian government was cooperating with PULO. PULO statements about alleged MCP arrangements with the Thai military also served to erode trust between Malaysian and Thai officials.

Publicly, Bangkok and Kuala Lumpur have downplayed reports of tension between them resulting from PULO and MCP activities. The author's discussions in Kuala Lumpur during a May 1981 visit, however, confirmed a general impression that the Malaysian government acquiesces in PULO activities in order to maintain links with southern Thai Muslims in case Vietnam should succeed in destabilizing Thailand sometime in the future. Moreover, Malaysian analysts believe the Thai government similarly avoids wholehearted cooperation in ousting the MCP from southern Thailand, viewing it as an ally against PULO activities.[90]

Indonesia, under military leadership, has delayed recognition of China because of the belief that the PRC—if it re-establishes a diplomatic presence—will use it to revitalize the PKI and subvert some three million Sino-Indonesian citizens. Although there is no evidence to suggest either that the Chinese business community is procommunist or that it would work for the PRC's interests, the military's experience with two major communist rebellions since Indonesia's independence has rendered it irreversibly suspicious of the Chinese and unwilling to provide Beijing any opportunity for re-entry into the country's affairs. Thus, when in November 1978 Deng Xiaoping stated that China could not publicly renounce its ties with the region's communist parties, Indonesian authorities seized the opportunity to announce that this position prevented normalization of relations with Jakarta.[91]

The only other insurgency that has benefited from external aid is the

Moro Rebellion in the Philippines. This uprising is not supported by external communist powers, however, but rather by an extra-regional militant Muslim state—Libya—and at times by the federated Malaysian state of Sabah. Moro Liberation Front Chairman Nur Misauri and a coterie of his followers have long been based in Tripoli, and the rebels have been armed via Sabah with Libyan and more recently Iranian financial support.[92] Nevertheless, the Moros present no threat to the central government. Adroit Philippine diplomacy has elicited political support from Manila's two Muslim partners, Malaysia and Indonesia. Both support Philippine integrity in Islamic forums since they, too, are wary of potential ethnic and separatist threats in their own countries.

The communist New People's Army (NPA) in Luzon, while still active, does not seem to be receiving outside aid. Both China and Vietnam have abjured interference in Philippine domestic affairs. NPA strength depends on domestic disaffection (which is growing) rather than outside nourishment. If communist strength grows, however, opportunities for renewed outside aid lurk in the wings, as does a possible linkup with the Moros in the south.

Border Insurgencies and Ethnic Minority Issues

In addition to problems arising from external aid to insurgent movements within ASEAN, domestic conditions also contribute to instability in the ASEAN area, particularly among rural ethnic minority and tribal groups whose cultures differ from that of the dominant political elite in urban centers and among those living in border regions who are attracted by irredentist appeals. Insofar as development is based on foreign investment and export-led growth, as it is in most ASEAN countries, growth tends to be concentrated in the cities. Thus, economic disparities reinforce regional, ethnic, and linguistic differences. It appears that only a relatively small portion of the population in ASEAN benefits from growth. This could endanger future regional stability, even in the absence of outside communist stimulation. Poverty is endemic in rain-fed northeastern Thailand. Its landless peasants and jobless laborers survive on the periphery of the modern economy, reaping virtually none of its benefits. This, combined with the fact that most of the region's inhabitants are Lao mountain tribesmen, translates into antipathy toward the central government. Not only do they resent the government's taxes and proscription of smuggling and opium growing, but they also believe that it provides no voice for their representatives. Indeed, all ASEAN governments are essentially authoritarian, a form justified as essential to control subversion and provide the kind of stability needed to attract foreign investment. To stay in power they depend upon the educated and military segments of the society who reside in the cities. Thus, the economic gap between rural and urban areas grows over time. Social services, such as education and health care, are located in the cities. Moreover, agricultural prices are kept artificially low to hold down the urban cost of living.[93]

At times this discrimination is particularly galling because it is so blatant. In Thailand, for example, Meos have been denied the right to acquire title to the land they farm; and Bangkok has encouraged lowland Thais to move into traditional Meo areas. Small wonder that some Meo are attracted to the CPT.[94] Bangkok has cause for concern over the potential disintegration of its hinterland in the north and northeast and even, to a degree, in the south. Unless the capital's Western commercial orientation can generate and then transfer resources to these areas to improve job opportunities and living standards, the Thai government may have to become increasingly repressive to control these regions. This, in turn, could have the paradoxical effect of generating more border uprisings, making the country at large less attractive to foreign investors. In short, rural development is probably the best long-term investment for political stability, which in turn is essential for the foreign investment required for urban progress. As Bruce Grant, a former Western diplomat and longtime observer of Southeast Asia, put it in a recent monograph: "By emphasizing the issue of security, based on the need for stability to protect foreign investment, rather than concentrating on political reconciliation and long-term rural improvements, Thailand may have played into the hands of her adversaries."[95]

All three major Thai insurgencies—the north, northeast, and south—though involving different ethnic groups, are based on similar grievances toward Bangkok. All ask for agricultural reform (particularly title to land that is farmed by local residents), low-cost credit, a more equitable judicial system, more regional development assistance, and a decentralized system of local administration. Allocation to rural reform of only a small portion of the resources expended on paramilitary control of these regions would probably benefit the government's pacification efforts considerably. General Prem has recognized this problem and plans to allocate new resources to agricultural development for the 1982–83 fiscal year and to raise prices for farm produce for the first time in several years.

Respect for local cultures is also a major political issue in Thailand's policies toward the insurgencies. The problems of the Meos are mentioned above. In the south, efforts at forced assimilation since the late 1950s designed to change the Muslim community's social fabric to make it more compatible with that of Thai Buddhists have generated resentment. Muslim elders object to governmental insistence that Thai curricula be used in Islamic schools as an attempt to steer young Muslims away from the faith. Moreover, some 70 percent of the instructors in the state schools of the region are Buddhist.

Resentment against Buddhist dominance in education has been translated into arson, kidnapping, extortion, and even murder. Some ten state schools were destroyed by arsonists in the southern district of Narathiwat in 1979, and in one particularly gruesome incident in Pattani, two Buddhist teachers were executed in front of their pupils.

Since only 3 percent of the students at Pattani University and less than 30 percent at Yala Teachers' College are Muslim, it is unlikely that Muslim teachers are being trained to assume the majority of educational positions in the region. The language barrier between the two communities complicates the situation even further; few Thai officials learn Malay and only about half the Muslim population speaks Thai. Civil service reforms reserving a limited number of university slots for Muslims who wish to join the civil service are too recent to have affected the number of Muslims working for the government. In early 1980, none of the 10 district officers and only 7 of the 50 assistant district officers in Narathiwat were Muslim.[96]

Even some of the government's self-help schemes for the region have backfired. Resettlement has encouraged the migration of landless Thai Buddhist farmers from the arid northeast. The Muslims view this as internal colonization—comparable to Moro complaints in the southern Philippines.

The chief worry for the future, however, lies with the activities of several thousand Thai Muslim students who have been educated abroad and returned. Unable to find suitable jobs in their home regions largely because of government suspicions of their intentions, they have begun to politicize the population and could well become the leadership nucleus of a new insurgency with both moral and material support from across the Malaysian border.

Some new wrinkles have developed in the CPT-directed insurgencies of the northeast and mid-south. Though the least publicized, the latter is potentially the most dangerous because of its proximity to Bangkok and the involvement of lowland Thais rather than ethnic minorities. Only in 1979 did the government begin to concentrate on this insurgency, whose bases are well hidden in the mountains and jungles of the region. Typically, the regime has treated the insurgents as a military problem, employing two army regiments and a battalion of marines.

Reports from the mid-south indicate that the CPT has become much less doctrinaire in its relations with the populace. The party concen-

trates on local grievances and assists villagers against corrupt local officials, who are bought off by the owners of the region's rich tin mines
and rubber plantations. The poor increasingly experience a sense of relative deprivation since district officials collect taxes from them but do
little to assess the wealth accumulating in the hands of plantation and
mine owners. As of 1979, there were no governmental development
projects in the mid-south to provide jobs for landless laborers. In contrast, such projects have been initiated in other insurgent regions. Since
recent highway building in the area is designed more to facilitate military movements than to improve market transportation, its impact on
the local economy has been negligible. Some observers believe that economic opporutnities in the mid-south will expand only with the planned
development of a new port at Songkhla along with connecting railroads
into the interior.[97]

The Vietnamese invasion of Cambodia appears to have transformed
CPT activities in the northeast, too. As the party lost its sanctuaries in
Laos, its cadres on the Thai side of the border shifted from an irredentist
orientation to an emphasis on Thai rural values. The party openly con-
demns Vietnamese imperialism and has offered to cooperate with government forces in defending Thailand. A close American observer of
CPT activities stated that the party has adopted a new conservative
cultural appeal for the restoration of rural values to replace the modern,
Western values of Bangkok capitalists, who have sold Thailand to the
imperialists. The party has decided to stay primarily in the rural areas for
the time being. Its Thai People's Liberation Army (TPLA) has an estimated 12,000–14,000 combatants, giving it the capability to harass government forces. The TPLA seems to have little difficulty in recruiting
sufficient new blood to replace its losses.[98]

In sum, it cannot be said that the Thai government has controlled the
country's disparate insurgencies. For the past fifteen years, they have
grown slowly, as have the military resources applied by Bangkok against
them. On the other hand, the insurgencies have not mushroomed in
size. They remain confined to rural areas, with a limited political appeal
to the majority of the Thai population. If a significant number of the
1,500 to 3,000 students who joined the insurgents after the 1976 military
coup choose to remain in the party, however, a new leadership cadre
could emerge with a more ethnic Thai orientation and, for the first time,
a potential urban base. But many of these students, disillusioned with
intraparty factionalism, a drop in PRC support, and the Vietnamese
threat to their nation, left the jungle in the early 1980s and rallied to the
government.

Malaysia must also cope with a significant insurgent problem, although rioting in 1969 demonstrated that Kuala Lumpur's long-term security was threatened less by the MCP than by the problems of communal cooperation between Chinese and Malay. Chinese domination of the Malaysian economy (and to a degree Indonesia's as well) forms the basis for racial resentment. A 1972–73 survey showed the Chinese owning 20 percent of the coconut and tea acreage while the Malays held none and 26 percent of the rubber trees and oil palms against 21 percent for Malays. (The rest are in foreign hands.) The disparities in favor of the Chinese in trade and industry were much larger. Under current government policy, Malays are supposed to own 30 percent of equity capital in all businesses by the end of the 1980s. Most analysts view this as much too optimistic a figure. The Chinese, for their part, object to discrimination in higher education since *bumiputra* (Malay) students are given preferential access to upgrade their economic capabilities. Out of some 6,000 students accepted by Malaysian universities in 1978–79, only 1,000 were Chinese.[99]

The commercial dominance of the Chinese in Malaysia is part of a broader ASEAN pattern. One estimate places 60 percent of regional trade in the hands of ethnic Chinese. Foreign businesses prefer dealing with Chinese partners in ASEAN because of their regional networks and entrepreneurial skills. A University of Hong Kong specialist recently argued that the overseas Chinese possessed an abundance of the qualities critical for business success: (1) a propensity to accumulate capital, (2) a work ethic centered on diligence and systematic action, (3) an ability to cooperate with others, and (4) a capacity for innovation and an openness to change. The last characteristic is facilitated by the generally autocratic style of decision making in Chinese business, which leads to rapid decisions—unlike the Malay propensity for delay and compromise until consensus can be attained.[100]

Given government-sanctioned discrimination against the Chinese community, it is not surprising that the MCP's ethnic composition is predominantly Chinese. But because the peninsular insurgency is Chinese, it has been unable to break out of an encapsulated rural location along the Thai border where some 3,000 guerrillas receive sanctuary from ethnic Chinese communities inside Thailand in the Songkhla and Betong areas.

Two insurgencies operate in the Philippines. Although the Moro Rebellion has obtained the most publicity because of its ties to the international Muslim community (see above) and the persistent, low-level military action taken to contain it, Philippine authorities claim to be more concerned about the communist rebellion in Luzon spearheaded by the NPA. While the Muslim rebellion neither threatens the central government nor is interested in replacing it, the NPA has the overthrow of the Marcos regime as its primary goal. Moreover, NPA strength is growing in both Luzon and further south in Samar. It has been particularly successful in recruiting in the depressed sugar-growing areas as unemployed landless laborers increase in number.[101]

Although NPA operations in Luzon may be the most worrisome to Manila, it is the Moros who account for the bulk of the country's military expenditures—some 90 percent. Military containment of the southern Muslim insurgents has proven to be not only intractable but also the most inflationary item in the government's budget. One military officer with experience in the south, who lectures at the National Defense College, admitted to the author that the army's behavior in the region has been a considerable part of the problem. Conscripts sent to the area have been both uneducated and undisciplined.[102] The military provides virtually no training for civic action. In many ways, the military treats local Muslims either as the enemy or as prey. Some military units have even degenerated into outright banditry. The low social and educational background of enlisted men and some noncommissioned officers results from the ability of the affluent either to buy their way out of military service or to employ political influence to the same end.

Whatever the role of the military's behavior, the major political issue in the south centers on the Muslims' belief that northern Christians have moved into the region, taken Muslim land by refusing to honor indigenous land tenure customs, and then sold the land to large foreign plantations—particularly the Japanese. The Muslims see very little chance under the Marcos government of getting their land back. Leadership for their cause is provided by young radicals educated abroad in Islamic countries or in some cases in Manila. Either location makes them acutely aware of the disparity between their living standards and those of the Christian majority.

The Moro Rebellion exemplifies the difficulties ASEAN states have encountered in dealing fairly with minorities. As long as the Philippine government treats the Sulu archipelago more as a military than a political and social issue, reconciliation is unlikely, especially since Philippine Muslims have access to aid from the Arab Middle East. Although adroit Philippine diplomacy, with Malaysian and Indonesian assistance, has limited the amount of aid funneled to the insurgents, it is probable that unless the Arab states can be convinced that the lot of their Philippine coreligionists is improving, outside aid to the rebels will increase in the 1980s.

On the positive side, Marcos seems to have dealt with the citizenship issue of resident Chinese rather well. After normalizing relations with the PRC in 1975 and receiving assurance from Beijing that it would not supply material assistance to the NPA, the Philippine president liberalized naturalization procedures. In 1978, he decreed that the 23,000 Chinese applicants awaiting determination of their cases would automatically become citizens if they were at least eighteen years old and had been residents for a minimum of five years. Additionally, anyone starting a new industry would also be given citizenship.[103]

The Overseas Chinese issue is most intractable in Indonesia because the ruling military's fear of the Chinese dates to the PRC's support for the PKI during the years leading up to its abortive coup in 1965.[104] Because elements of the military elite involved in commercial ventures use the entrepreneurial skills of resident Chinese and their regional trading networks, the belief that all Chinese in Southeast Asia are somehow linked is reinforced. Fear that these linkages extend to Beijing accounts in large part for Indonesia's reluctance to re-establish diplomatic ties. Indonesia's leaders still view the country's three million Chinese as a potential fifth column.

Despite Indonesia's apprehensions about the Chinese, some two million have, in fact, already acquired citizenship. Only one million of a total population of about 140 million are aliens. Since 1978, a number of Indonesian officials have begun to rethink the Chinese citizenship problem. Becuase the government abrogated the 1960 Dual Nationality Treaty with the PRC in the wake of the PKI coup attempt, there is currently no legal instrument defining the status of resident Chinese who are not Indonesian citizens.

In the fall of 1979, the state intelligence coordinating body, Bakin, broached a plan to streamline citizenship application procedures so that naturalization could be completed in six months. The political rationale for this mass citizenship plan (which, procedurally, is similar to that of the Philippines) is that official discrimination toward the number of Chinese aliens makes them a ready target for PRC manipulation. As citizens with a stake in the country, however, their susceptibility to Beijing's appeals will diminish because they risk expulsion and the loss of their possessions if they allow themselves to be used by the PRC.[105]

Between 1967 and 1974, the lot of Chinese businesses improved greatly under Suharto's New Order. Concerned primarily with reviving the economy, the government supported established economic forces. The Chinese flourished in this environment, given their location in banking and manufacturing. By 1973, however, indigenous Indonesians (*pribumi*) perceived an imbalance in the private sector. They saw the Chinese receiving the lion's share of available credit and, even worse, squeezing out pribumi businesses. The issue came to a head in the riots of January 1974 in the Malari section of Jakarta. Ostensibly directed against visiting Japanese Prime Minister Tanaka Kakuei, in fact, the riots were a manifestation of the perceived lack of governmental support for indigenous businessmen.

By the late 1970s the government had altered its credit policy so that the largest category of borrowers was no longer Chinese (30 percent) but rather the pribumi (37 percent).[106] Moreover, government banks—controlled, of course, by pribumi—now extend over 80 percent of the country's credit, while private Chinese banks account for about 9 percent of the total. In contrast, the Chinese control between 50 and 60 percent of internal commerce.

The arena in which Chinese businessmen have done particularly well is less their own enterprises than in managing companies backed by government funds. Although the Chinese managers of these companies lack equity in them, they are paid handsome stipends to run the companies' affairs. Pribumi generals own the companies and obtain the licenses and grants necessary to do business, while the Chinese managers possess the skills and contacts to both manufacture and market the products.

Problems with assimilating ethnic minorities will persist in the ASEAN states for the foreseeable future. None threatens the political core of any given country, but almost all divert resources into such unproductive expenditures as military control (the Philippines, Malaysia, and Thailand). The problems cluster at both ends of the economic spectrum. At the low end, minority hill tribes in Thailand and Muslims in the Philippines see their patrimony taken from them with few compensatory opportunities for improvement. These people become prime candidates for either indigenous or foreign-backed rebellions. At the other end of the spectrum are the Chinese, who dominate private trade and credit facilities in several of the ASEAN states. They have encountered discrimination with respect to educational opportunities (Malaysia and Indonesia) and citizenship (Indonesia and the Philippines). Full legal equality for resident Chinese is essential to harness their talents and energies for national development goals. In sum, disproportionate economic assistance to border area and tribal minorities and political equality for ASEAN's Chinese citizens would promote regional stability since these policies would help eliminate the conditions that may tempt these groups to view government as an adversary and to seek outside aid against it.

3 | *ASEAN* COOPERATION

Problems, conflicts, and challenges to the viability of states may also provide opportunities for cooperation. ASEAN can effectively meet many of the challenges outlined in the preceding chapter only through such cooperation. This chapter explores the experiences in political cooperation of the Association's members and assesses their effects on regional security and the development of an ASEAN-wide sense of political community.

ASEAN's first major political commitment to security cooperation came with the 1976 Bali concord, which provided for "continuation of cooperation on a non-ASEAN basis between the member-states on security matters in accordance with their mutual needs and interests." Although not a security organization itself, ASEAN can be regarded as an umbrella under which the five member-states may engage in bi- or multilateral security activities. ASEAN's caution about security activities, which seems to be dissipating as Vietnamese belligerence increases, grew out of the concern that the Association not be seen as "son of SEATO." Not long after Hanoi's invasion of Cambodia, however, representatives from Thailand, Singapore, Malaysia, and Indonesia began to discuss possible military cooperation in the face of Vietnam's new challenge.[1] A changed, more threatening regional environment may be modifying ASEAN's reluctance to operate as a security group. The Association now openly opposes Vietnamese and Soviet moves in the region and has attempted to enlist the support of other Third World countries.

Border Region Cooperation

Precedents for the current readiness to discuss security date back almost to the Association's founding. Bilateral border security cooperation was standard through the 1970s between Indonesia and Malaysia and Malaysia and Thailand, including joint patrols and coordinated field actions against the MCP. The Indonesian government maintained that such operations did not constitute a military alliance because they were directed not against a foreign country but rather against "subversive elements."[2] Similarly the 1976 Thai-Malaysian border agreement—the most extensive institutionalization of joint military action between two ASEAN states—provides for a combined task force headquarters and combined as well as unilateral operations. The agreement even gives the military forces of each state the right of hot pursuit into the other's territory. Both governments assured their people that the agreement did not violate national sovereignty or constitute a military alliance.[3] During this same period, Indonesia and Malaysia reached a comparable joint military arrangement to control subversive elements operating along their Borneo jungle border. At that time Malaysian Minister of Home Affairs Ghazali Shafie stated there was no need for a major American military presence in Southeast Asia "because we do not expect an invasion . . . Our insurgencies we can handle with cooperative arrangements among ourselves."[4] At the time, the prognosis seemed accurate. Vietnam had not donated any of its captured U.S. arsenal to regional insurgents, and both China and the Soviet Union were competing for ASEAN's favor.

The ASEAN countries are particularly conscious of the potential for mischief inherent in secessionist movements in their border regions. There is a mutual interest in discouraging such movements anywhere in the region even if the actions taken to suppress them meet with international disapproval. For example, the other four ASEAN states provided diplomatic support for Indonesia's policy regarding integration of Timor and the military suppression of dissidents despite West European protests. Both Malaysia and Indonesia have assisted the Philippines in defusing the international opprobrium in the Muslim community over suppression of the Moro Rebellion.

Joint actions have not always been easy for ASEAN states, however, even on a bilateral basis. The absence of a common language and differences in terminology hampered Thai-Malaysian operations against the MCP just inside the Thai border in 1978. When the Malaysians said "logistics," the Thais were lost since they use the term "resources control." When the Thais spoke of "masses orientation," the Malaysians did not understand that it meant "civic action." Moreover, operations of one nation's army on the other's territory led to confusion because the order of battle varied.[5] Moreover, joint actions that appear to benefit only one participant may cause resentment in the other partner's country. Military operations in southern Thailand have helped primarily Malaysia since their object is the MCP. Some Thais are concerned not only that the benefit has flowed in one direction but also that the extensive use of military force, including air and artillery, has alienated much of the local population from the Thai government. In effect, Thailand may be incurring a net political loss from its cooperation with Malaysia in the southern border region.[6]

The Soviets (and probably their Vietnamese allies) view security efforts among the ASEAN countries with considerable distaste. ASEAN security cooperation precludes interest in the Moscow-sponsored Asian collective security treaty. Moscow and Hanoi also see the various ASEAN bilateral security arrangements as a revitalization of SEATO and fear that over time, the ASEAN states would move from joint military actions to the standardization of military equipment and doctrine. ASEAN would then be prepared to provide ground defense for the region (in line with the Nixon Doctrine), which the United States would complement with air and naval support from its Pacific bases and the Seventh Fleet.[7]

Malaysia and Thailand may reassess their antiguerrilla operations in the early 1980s. Most important for Bangkok is that both the source and imminence of the threat to its integrity changed dramatically with the Vietnamese invasion of Cambodia and the subsequent presence of thousands of VPA regulars along the Thai border. Whereas Thailand had built a military in the 1970s on the premise that its primary concern would be domestic insurgency, in 1980 that army confronted the prospect of conventional military invasion by the best-equipped force in the region. The question facing the military concerns its ability to defend Thailand against Vietnamese incursions and the kind of assistance it can expect to receive from both the United States and its ASEAN partners. The security challenge to Thailand may be the litmus test for any future security coordination by ASEAN members. (This issue is examined more closely below.)

Security cooperation along the Thai border has been Malaysia's primary military activity since the signing of the current security arrangement with Bangkok in 1976. Since 1977, a series of coordinated border operations kept the MCP on the run but neither reduced its strength (around 2,000) nor led to larger numbers of slain or captured insurgents or to increases in the number of surrenders. In 1978 and 1979, according to Malaysian security officials, a total of 71 MCP and CPT members were killed in the border operations, 18 were captured, and 55 capitulated. These are not impressive body counts, especially when compared with Malaysia's military and police budgets for internal security of M $330 million (approximately U.S. $130 million) for 1979, most of which goes into border control.[8]

Malaysia has initiated some development programs for its depressed northern states of Kedah, Perlis, Kelantan, and Trengganu. A highway is being built across northern Malaysia from Penang on the west coast to Kota Bharu on the east coast to help open thousands of acres to agriculture. Thailand has begun development projects on its side of the border. A joint "security and development committee" is coordinating these programs.[9]

Because Thailand has had to focus its attention along the Cambodian and Laotian borders, since 1979 the initiative for military actions in the southern part of the country has devolved on the Malaysians. Thailand has let Malaysia manage the "back door" while it barricades the "front door."[10] The hot-pursuit clause permits Malaysian forces to operate with more flexibility on Thai soil than ever before, though most Malaysian forays have been concentrated in the Betong salient against MCP sanctuaries. A major, 10,000-men Malaysian force swept through the area between October 1979 and January 1980. Reports from Bangkok, however, suggest that it may be the last for some time.

The Thai government is increasingly sensitive to charges that Malaysian forces are roaming at will in the south, and Bangkok may also be concerned over reports of fraternization between Malaysian soldiers and Thai Muslim separatists.[11] Whatever the reason, Thai officials have called a halt to large-scale joint operations. The new tactics call for an increase in local intelligence gathering, long-range self-contained patrols to ferret out insurgent locations, and only then the calling in of company-size mobile strike forces. "Before, we used large forces to hammer them, and we needed a lot of supplies," a Thai military planner stated. "Now we are thinking in terms of an economy of force."[12]

Given the locus of these operations on Thai soil, Malaysia has little choice but to defer to Bangkok's wishes. Its military is not pleased, however. It believes that large-scale operations had kept the MCP on the run. Malaysia, for its part, has extended very little cooperation to Thailand in helping to control the Thai Muslim separatist movement. Thai forces, for example, do not have reciprocal rights of hot pursuit into

Malaysian territory. Malaysian intelligence has not provided Bangkok with information on the Muslim dissidents—reportedly because the latter have been an excellent source of information about the MCP.[13] As yet, this lack of cooperation has not become a point of contention because the Thai Muslim problem remains fairly low level. But three separatist organizations exist in the Thai south and could become more troublesome in the future. During 1979, separatist-bandit incidents exceeded those caused by the MCP, although this may reflect the large military operations launched against the latter during this period.

In 1981 new strains occurred over Thai-Malaysian border control. Malaysian reports of Thai military cooperation with the MCP to suppress PULO guerrillas in the Betong salient paralleled private Thai intelligence accusations that PULO and the Malaysian military had a working relationship for the purpose of monitoring MCP activities in Thailand. If accurate, these reports portend new trouble for Thai-Malaysian security cooperation at a time when Bangkok must increasingly rely on Malaysian assistance to control their joint border.[14]

Other ASEAN states cooperate with respect to vulnerable borders and insurgent control, although no other arrangement is as well articulated as the Thai-Malaysian. Malaysia and Indonesia coordinate military actions along their Sarawak border in Borneo, but neither allows the other border-crossing privileges. The small number of terrorists—estimated to be about 300—hardly warrants full-blown joint efforts.[15]

By early 1977, a series of agreements between Thailand and the Philippines, the Philippines and Singapore, and Thailand and Malaysia led to the exchange of security intelligence and regular discussions of subversion and insurgency. An interlocking network of bilateral intelligence cooperation is virtually complete. Indonesian and Filipino armed forces have long collaborated, as have the intelligence organs of Malaysia and Singapore. There is one possible exception. The Filipino armed forces may still be suspicious of Malaysia's intentions because of Malaysian assistance to the Moro Rebellion in the past.

Maritime security cooperation is also based on a series of joint agreements:

Philippines and Indonesia. Joint naval exercises beginning in 1975. Joint sea patrol agreement in 1975 denying sanctuary to those involved in illegal activities in either state.

Singapore and Indonesia. Agreement in 1974 to patrol jointly the Straits of Malacca and Singapore against smugglers. Naval exercises beginning in 1975.

Malaysia-Indonesia-Thailand. Agreement to conduct joint patrols against smuggling, gunrunning, and piracy in the Strait of Malacca.

Thailand and Indonesia. Agreement to conduct joint naval exercises leading to the policing of the upper part of the Strait of Malacca.

A limited exchange of military training occurs. Some Singaporean and Malaysian air force personnel train in Thailand; Indonesian officers train in Malaysia; the Philippines has provided an island for Singaporean infantry maneuvers. Malaysia, however, still refuses Singapore access to its jungle training center in Johore—a legacy from the mid-1960s when Kuala Lumpur asked the city-state to leave the federation for fear of Lee Kwan Yew's political ambitions.

The ASEAN states have virtually no plans to standardize military equipment. In September 1978, Thailand and Singapore agreed to a joint venture in light-arms production, but it was capitalized at only U.S. $1.83 million.[16] Most ASEAN military equipment is purchased from the West, particularly the United States. Nevertheless, despite common supply sources, ASEAN armies have coordinated neither weapons systems purchases, logistics arrangements, nor military doctrine. Each of the five sees its military tasks as sui generis, concerned primarily with domestic challenges. Cooperation with neighbors remains a secondary interest and almost exclusively bilateral. Although government planners recognize the potential for a regionwide security challenge by Vietnam with Soviet backing, no apparent changes occurred in 1980 in joint military consultation or in weapons procurement. In sum, there were no military developments paralleling the careful, coordinated political exchanges that had evolved to cope with Vietnam's challenge to ASEAN. Military procurement, exercises, and deployment remained at the same level as during the preceding decade.

The Vietnamese Challenge

The catalyst for ASEAN's newfound political coordination has been the threat of a new regional hegemonic state with ties to a hostile superpower. Although initially hoping to cajole Vietnam after 1975 into a productive relationship centered on ASEAN assistance for its economic recovery, the Association's incentives proved insufficient to deflect Hanoi's ambition away from regional dominance. As the SRV consolidated its ties to the USSR, first through membership in COMECON and then through a security pact in 1978, ASEAN's hopes for Soviet and Vietnamese support for ZOPFAN evaporated.

Actually, Vietnam had displayed some hostility toward Thailand almost throughout the post–Indochinese war period, castigating Bangkok's efforts to control its northern border insurgencies and condemning cooperative arrangements with Malaysia to do the same in the south. The SRV attempt to drive a wedge between Thailand and the other ASEAN members appeared to be succeeding. Bangkok's neighbors ignored its hints about the desirability of some ASEAN assistance in its anti-insurgent activities. All feared antagonizing Vietnam, with its considerable military potential; because none shared a border with the SRV, they chose to view Thailand's security concerns as a domestic Thai problem rather than a regional one.

Premier Pham Van Dong's September–October 1978 visits to ASEAN capitals were designed to sustain a mood of quiescence. Vietnamese pledges not to assist regional insurgencies were warmly received. Each state, however, rejected Hanoi's offer of bilateral nonaggression pacts and friendship treaties. In retrospect these rejections constituted a watershed in ASEAN's political development; a meeting of ASEAN officials in Bangkok prior to Dong's visit had agreed that no treaties or agreements would be initialed with Vietnam for fear that China would view these as a first step in drawing ASEAN into a Soviet-Vietnamese-led entente. To underline the ASEAN five's independence, the joint statements issued in Bangkok, Manila, Jakarta, and Kuala Lumpur all included stipulations pledging continued ASEAN aspirations for the realization of ZOPFAN. By implication, of course, this meant a region free from outside military interference.[17]

Even after the Vietnamese occupation of Cambodia, ASEAN leaders publicly expressed optimism regarding future relations. Thai Foreign Minister Pachariyangkun Uppadit's comments were typical:

> Vietnam is facing an economic depression due to the aftermath of the war. It has to launch a rehabilitation program which may take ten to 20 years. Besides, Vietnam also has . . . problems with Cambodia, draining its resources which should have been used for economic rehabilitation. That's why I think Vietnam doesn't want to be an enemy of Thailand.

Additionally, Uppadit warned: "The five ASEAN member countries have a combined population of 250 million people and possess abundant natural resources. If Vietnam should become an enemy of Thailand, it will also have problems with other ASEAN countries."[18]

As Vietnam consolidated its position in Cambodia and China

encroached on Vietnam's border provinces, it became clear to ASEAN that the new Indochinese hostilities were part of both Sino-Vietnamese and Sino-Soviet tensions. While it was unlikely that ASEAN could do much to ameliorate these tensions, regular and frequent meetings to effect a united front toward both adversarial camps were imperative. Not to do so would risk the possibility of a political split and alignment with the competitors.

The ASEAN states have tried to mediate between China and Vietnam, despite past statements that such mediation efforts were outside the ASEAN framework. There was general agreement within ASEAN councils that the only possible way to defuse Sino-Vietnamese hostilities over Cambodia while restoring Thai security would be to convince Vietnam to withdraw its forces in exchange for a neutral coalition government pledged to maintain correct relations with both Vietnam and China. The Association hoped the Russians might find this solution acceptable because they would retain their political and military ties with Vietnam while the potential for war by miscalculation over Cambodia would be greatly reduced.[19] ASEAN was particularly wary of any new Chinese attack on Vietnam that might be rationalized as a contribution to Thailand's defense. Any such move could be interpreted as drawing Thailand to the Chinese side in the Sino-Vietnamese conflict and hence undermine ASEAN neutrality.

The Chinese connection is the crux of ASEAN's political problem. Because Thailand has tolerated shipment of Chinese military assistance to the Khmer Rouge through Thai territory and because the PRC's deployment of forces along Hanoi's northern border relieves the military pressure on the Cambodian border, Beijing is, in fact, a tacit ally of Thailand. Bangkok cannot acknowledge the relationship, however, since ASEAN sees its long-term security in regional neutrality rather than in alignment with either China or the SRV and the USSR. This desire to avoid being entangled in the Sino-Vietnamese hostilities is particularly important since there is no consensus within ASEAN concerning which of the two adversaries is the greater threat to the region. While Thailand, Singapore, and, to a lesser extent, the Philippines see Vietnam in that role, Indonesia and Malaysia are openly fearful of the potential for mischief in a resurgent China.

Hanoi's diplomacy toward ASEAN displays considerable ambivalence, alternating between "carrot" and "stick" tactics. For example, when the boat people phenomenon elicited cries of outrage from the ASEAN countries of first asylum in 1979, Hanoi may have tried to ameliorate the negative impact by dropping its vehement opposition to Thai-Malaysian cooperation against the MCP. Suddenly Hanoi acknowledged that this was an "internal affair" of the two states, perhaps in the hope that ASEAN might reciprocate with respect to Hanoi's actions toward its own "undesirables."[20] If this was the case, Hanoi was to be sadly disappointed.

Instead of merely looking on helplessly, the ASEAN states struck back diplomatically. The Bali Foreign Ministers' Conference in July 1979 condemned the refugee flow not only as inhumane but also as an attempt to destabilize the region by disrupting its ethnic balance. The Association projected the refugee flow as an opening gambit in an ominous SRV plan to foment instability as a prerequisite to invasion—with Thailand the first target. The foreign ministers agreed that any threat to Thailand would be a threat to all of ASEAN and urged Vietnam to defuse the situation by withdrawing its forces from Cambodia.[21]

Noteworthy here was ASEAN agreement to defer to the preferences of its most threatened member, the country that had most at stake in the conflict. All countries at the Bali meeting—with the exception of the Philippines—pledged military support to Thailand if necessary. While these symbolic gestures were gratefully received in Bangkok, they were not proffered entirely for altruistic reasons. The other ASEAN states feared the possibility of Thailand's turning to China. Their expressions of support were designed to demonstrate that Thailand had regional backing and did not stand alone. To help Thailand, ASEAN has stated that Vietnam must prove its good intentions by removing VPA troops from Cambodia. And ASEAN diplomacy has had some impact. The nonaligned countries have followed ASEAN's lead in the United Nations, for example, with respect to denying membership to the Hanoi-backed Heng Samrin regime. Until July 1980, when India broke ranks, no noncommunist state had recognized the government in Phnom Penh. Similarly, the United States, Japan, Australia, New Zealand, and the EEC countries all seem to be following ASEAN's lead on Cambodian developments. The foreign ministers of these industrial states now meet regularly with their ASEAN counterparts after the latters' conclaves to coordinate diplomatic positions in the Southeast Asian conflict.

Thailand's call in the U.N. General Assembly for an international peace force for Cambodia elicited an angry rebuttal from Hanoi that Bangkok had "joined the imperialists in their wars of aggression against Vietnam, Laos, and Kampuchea. If Thailand persists in its past mistakes by maintaining a hostile attitude to the peoples of Indochina, it will do damage to its own interest and will harm peace and stability in Southeast Asia."[22] Singapore's particularly barbed comments have resulted in blatantly racist commentaries by SRV media. Typical is the following:

"The reactionary allegations of the Singaporean authorities and those of the Beijing rulers are completely identical, so much so that one should wonder whether the Singaporean authorities now still represent an independent country in Southeast Asia."[23] Not to be outdone, Singapore's U.N. ambassador, T. T. Koh, openly accused the Vietnamese of a "clear contravention of certain assurances" given to ASEAN leaders in 1978 that Hanoi would not interfere in other countries' affairs. How could these assurances be reconciled with Vietnam's invasion of Cambodia? Koh asked.[24]

While verbal fireworks exploded at the United Nations, private discussion indicated that ASEAN was seriously searching for a solution to the Cambodia situation, which, it was hoped, could reconcile the security interests of Thailand and Vietnam—if not China. Thai officials admitted that they were fighting not so much for the recognition of Pol Pot's regime—about which all ASEAN members held severe reservations—but rather for world support for the neutralization of Cambodia. To recognize Heng Samrin would undermine the ASEAN cause, for it would not only legitimate Vietnamese aggression but also tacitly acknowledge Vietnam's control over Indochina, eliminating an historical buffer between Thailand and its traditional enemy.

ASEAN officials accept the proposition that even if Vietnam were willing to accommodate the Association's wishes, it could not pull out of Cambodia precipitously. The infrastructure created since January 1979 for the day-to-day survival of the country is totally dependent on the Vietnamese presence. Moreover, ASEAN also recognizes the impossibility of Vietnamese acceptance of an alternative regime that would be either anti-Vietnamese or pro-Beijing. The Association understands that, therefore, Vietnam cannot simply leave Cambodia, for this would precipitate open warfare by the Khmer Rouge as they attempted to retake control. A Vietnamese exit under these conditions would be the formula for a terrible bloodbath. The first step toward a solution, according to ASEAN thinking, would be to put a U.N. force in place as the Vietnamese withdraw. The United Nations could then supervise some sort of elections after a suitable period of time had elapsed and the situation inside the country had been restored to "normalcy."

ASEAN's proposal has been endorsed by the Khmer Rouge, who see it as their only viable prospect for a return to power, but it begs as many questions as it purports to answer. How would political groups organize themselves to appeal to an electorate? How would they be funded? Would the United Nations, as the responsible authority replacing Vietnam, agree to subsidize Cambodia for an extended period? (Estimates suggest it may cost Hanoi and Moscow between $1 and $2 million per day to sustain the SRV's presence in the country—although military hardware rather than welfare expenditures for the population accounts for much of that sum.)

Vietnamese officials recognize their own dilemma in occupying Cambodia. As Politburo member Le Duc Tho admitted in an interview with the French Communist Party paper, L'Humanité, the longer Vietnamese forces remain on Cambodian soil the more likely it is that they will be seen as conquerors rather than liberators.[25] But, at the same time, to leave would be unthinkable since a Vietnamese withdrawal would be followed by the return of the only organized opposition force in Cambodia—the PRC-backed Khmer Rouge. In effect, this would mean that China would have succeeded in virtually surrounding Vietnam.

The implications of Vietnam's strategic thinking are both clear and depressing to ASEAN. No Vietnamese withdrawal from Cambodia can occur until the SRV and China agree on a modus vivendi. This means that China would have to stop using the Khmer Rouge to bleed Vietnam and accept Hanoi's de facto supremacy in Indochina. Even if the Soviet Union were not on Vietnam's side, this would be a bitter pill for China to swallow. But with Hanoi so closely aligned to Moscow, acceptance of Vietnam's Indochina hegemony is unthinkable to Chinese leaders. Soviet-aligned Indochina would go far toward the realization of Brezhnev's Asian collective security proposal, particularly since it would be buttressed on the west by Russian-occupied Afghanistan and an India, once again under Indira Gandhi, that leans toward Soviet leadership in the region in exchange for economic and military assistance as well as diplomatic support in its territorial disputes with China. It is the potential linkage among these Soviet bilateral relationships that China fears. A prime goal of Chinese diplomacy is to convince ASEAN not to capitulate to Hanoi (and Moscow) so that Southeast Asia will not be added to what China perceives to be a growing Soviet bloc of Third World states:

> The armed Soviet occupation of Afghanistan is posing a direct threat to the oil-producing Gulf region and the oil lanes of Western Europe, Japan, and the United States. If the Soviet Union continues its westward thrust from Afghanistan to Iran and the Arabian Peninsula and its eastward thrust to South Asia while using Vietnam to expand from Indochina to Southeast Asia, the Strait of Malacca—the passageway between the Pacific and Indian Oceans—will be caught in a pincer attack from the east

and west. Upon completing this step, the Soviet Union will be in a position to control the Middle East, the Persian Gulf, Southeast Asia and the Strait of Malacca, and its strategic deployment for world hegemony will be basically completed.[26]

In an effort to make the Khmer Rouge more palatable both to ASEAN and world opinion generally, Beijing persuaded its leaders to remove Pol Pot as prime minister and to state that any Khmer Rouge government in authority after a Vietnamese withdrawal "will agree immediately to sign a treaty of friendship and peaceful coexistence with Vietnam." Further, Khieu Samphan, the new prime minister, pledged that no country would be permitted to set up military bases in Cambodia.[27] In short, a Khmer Rouge government could maintain good relations with Vietnam and ASEAN need not search for an alternative. Displaying even more flexibility, PRC spokesmen agreed in 1981 that a new coalition be effected between the noncommunist resistance led by former Premier Son Sann and Prince Sihanouk and the Khmer Rouge. A combined leadership for the resistance would help to secure continued international recognition in the United Nations and obstruct acceptance of the Heng Samrin regime.

Not to be outdone, Vietnam also attempted to portray its newly established "confederation" as salutary for the region's security. A foreign ministers' conference of the three Indochinese states, held in Phnom Penh in January 1980, pledged their willingness to negotiate nonaggression pacts with other countries in Southeast Asia.[28] Thailand has been particularly wary of these Vietnamese diplomatic gambits and their potential for splitting ASEAN's united front. Bangkok's ambassador in Hanoi asked that any visits to ASEAN states by high-level Vietnamese be conducted on a country-by-country basis so that ASEAN would have the opportunity to consult about the implications of any discussion at the end of each trip and before the beginning of the next.[29]

Thailand's concern over ASEAN differences was clearly warranted. In late March 1980, the leaders of the two member-states least enthusiastic about the "China connection" met in Kuantan, Malaysia—President Suharto of Indonesia and Prime Minister Hussein of Malaysia. Two days of discussion resulted in the Kuantan principle for solving the Thai-Indochina confrontation (see above). The Kuantan principle implicitly rejected China's policy of bleeding Vietnam white and attempted to reintroduce ZOPFAN by pointing out to the SRV that Hanoi had to alter its alignment if the region's independence was to be maintained.[30]

A senior Malaysian official explained that Indonesia and Malaysia believed that the SRV now realized suppression of the Khmer Rouge would be a protracted and expensive operation, particularly since Khmer Rouge strength appeared to have increased to between 30,000 and 40,000 military personnel by 1980. If Vietnam accepted the Kuantan principle and withdrew its forces from the Thai border, ASEAN would recognize Hanoi's Heng Samrin regime in Cambodia and, by implication, Thailand would cease supporting the Khmer Rouge.

This Indonesian-Malaysian gambit failed to win acceptance for several reasons. First, it represents the views of the two ASEAN states most pro-Vietnam and anti-China. Both Malaysia and Indonesia believe China to be the greater long-term threat to Southeast Asia but have agreed to subordinate this strategic view because Vietnam presents a clear and present danger to Thailand—ASEAN's front-line state. Nevertheless, Kuala Lumpur and Jakarta are committed to a political solution that accepts Hanoi's pre-eminence in Indochina as a balance to any future Chinese ambitions. Thailand cannot agree with this view at present (although in a less tense environment it might). Second, Bangkok welcomes China's support for its resistance to Hanoi and its acceptance of thousands of Cambodian refugees. China is also indebted to Thailand for its willingness to permit the Thai-Cambodian border areas to be used as a resupply zone for the Khmer Rouge. In exchange, China sustains military pressure on Vietnam's northern border, forcing the VPA to split its resources. And third, for the time being at least, the PRC and Thailand have parallel interests. If, however, ASEAN devises a political settlement with Hanoi removing VPA forces from the Thai border, Bangkok might well alter its diplomacy to develop a new modus vivendi with the SRV. Part of this new arrangement could well be a cessation of Thailand's cooperation in aiding the Khmer Rouge. Not surprisingly, then, China opposes the Kuantan principle and argues that ASEAN not endorse it.

Official Thai reactions have been vague. Not wishing to insult its ASEAN partners, Bangkok has not openly rejected the ideas put forth in Kuantan. But Thai Foreign Minister Sitthi Sawetsila has insisted that Vietnamese troop withdrawal must be a *precondition* for any kind of political settlement. In what could be construed as a partial rejection of Kuantan, he also insisted that to be acceptable to Thailand, any government in Phnom Penh must be free of "foreign influence."[31]

China's reaction to Kuantan was less restrained. Foreign Minister Huang Hua warned that the withdrawal of Vietnamese forces from Cambodia must not be bartered for recognition of a Vietnamese puppet regime in Phnom Penh.[32] The Vietnamese, in contrast, have chosen to ignore the Kuantan gambit by simply insisting that since there is no

Cambodian problem, there need be no political solution.[33] As for the ASEAN belief that the Soviet Union constitutes a threat to Southeast Asia, SRV Foreign Minister Thach stated that the only threat comes from China, while Russian influence helps stabilize the region.[34]

From Hanoi's point of view the Kuantan resolution had one advantage—its potential for splitting ASEAN politically and perhaps isolating Thailand, the member-state most cooperative with Beijing. When asked whether the Kuantan statement represented a retreat from ASEAN's U.N. resolution calling for the withdrawal of Vietnamese troops from Cambodia, Prime Minister Hussein averred that ASEAN was still guided by that resolution, but its basic concern was the protection of Thailand's sovereignty and integrity. If Vietnam failed to honor the U.N. resolution, then other ways should be sought to protect Thailand—ergo, the Kuantan proposal.[35] One interpretation of Hussein's position was that ASEAN might be satisfied if Vietnam guaranteed not to challenge Thailand's sovereignty and territorial control. Previously, the ASEAN-sponsored U.N. resolution had insisted not only on the withdrawal of Vietnamese troops from Cambodia but also on internationally supervised elections.[36] Most disturbing from Bangkok's view was that Hussein was making these statements without consulting Thailand in advance, hence providing the SRV with an opportunity to split ASEAN's united front. One Thai paper bemoaned the differences among ASEAN states revealed by the Kuantan principle, pointing out that such differences strengthened Hanoi's intransigence:

> The reason for Vietnam's unswerving rejection of ASEAN's [U.N. resolution] is that Vietnam realizes that ASEAN states themselves view the problem from different stands. Indonesia and Malaysia are obviously afraid of threats from China. Moreover, Indonesia expresses sympathy with Vietnam in its conflict with China. This is why Vietnam adopts a rather aggressive reaction to ASEAN's proposal.[37]

Following the apparent disagreement among the ASEAN states in the wake of the Kuantan controversy, Hanoi initiated diplomatic feelers to explore the possible parameters of a new ASEAN-SRV relationship. Reiterating, in a late May 1980 visit to Bangkok, that Vietnamese forces would remain in Cambodia until the perceived threat from China ended, SRV Foreign Minister Thach stated that the countries of the region should turn to the question of how to set up a "zone of peace and stability." Such a zone, he elaborated, must acknowledge the solidarity of the three Indochina states just as it would accept the solidarity of the five members of ASEAN. This arrangement could then supersede the

U.N. resolution calling for the withdrawal of troops and a neutral Cambodia. After all, the SRV foreign minister observed: "We have no intention to make any of the five ASEAN countries a buffer zone between the two groups [ASEAN and Indochina]. So we cannot accept any proposal that any of these [Indochinese] states be made into a buffer zone."[38] Hanoi evidently hoped that this proposal would appeal to Malaysia and Indonesia and lead to an effort on their part to persuade their ASEAN associates to accept a somewhat reduced number of VPA forces in Cambodia just as the five have accepted some 40,000 VPA personnel in Laos. Soviet diplomats in Hanoi informed the Japanese that the SRV would pull its troops away from the Thai border as soon as China stopped aiding the Khmer Rouge.[39] All of these signals seem designed to exploit the not-so-latent differences between Thailand/Singapore as hard-liners and Malaysia/Indonesia as potential conciliators of Vietnam.

The SRV's efforts to split the Association encountered a severe setback, however, in late June 1980, when a VPA battalion penetrated Thai territory to disrupt border camps where the Thai army was organizing repatriation convoys. The Vietnamese undoubtedly feared that the repatriation of several thousand Cambodians into Khmer Rouge–controlled sections of the border region would serve to build up the latter's military forces during the rainy season when VPA military operations virtually cease.

At a special meeting of the ASEAN foreign ministers convened in Kuala Lumpur to address the Thai incursions, the united front against Hanoi solidified once again. The foreign ministers specifically noted that these "latest acts of aggression against Thailand have further undermined Vietnam's own credibility and have greatly diminished the trust and confidence which ASEAN has patiently attempted to forge with Vietnam." The foreign ministers further agreed that "any incursion of foreign forces into Thailand directly affects the security of the ASEAN member states."[40] ASEAN commentaries pointed to the parallel between Vietnam's thrust into Thailand after assurances that it would not cross that country's border and Vietnamese assurances in 1978 that Hanoi would not invade Cambodia. ASEAN's condemnation of the SRV action was quite explicit. For the first time it identified Vietnam by name as the aggressor (instead of referring to "foreign powers").

The hard-line Thailand/Singapore position, therefore, dominated the meeting, leading to a temporary disruption of talks with the Vietnamese. Malaysia was clearly unhappy with these developments, arguing privately that Vietnam's belligerence made it all the more important to engage Hanoi in political efforts to break the impasse on the future of

Indochina.[41] Indonesian Foreign Minister Mochtar on returning from Malaysia said that discussions with Hanoi must continue, adding that despite the clashes with Thailand, bilateral relations between Jakarta and Hanoi remained good.[42]

Seizing these indications of concern about severing the dialogue with Vietnam, Hanoi media commented:

> We know that this communiqué does not adequately reflect all genuine views held by different ASEAN countries and that not all ASEAN politicians hold the same views as and act like a number of Thai politicians who falsely accuse Vietnam and assist the Pol Pot clique in hopes of winning a big gain ... We also know that not all ASEAN politicians act like some people within the Singaporean circles who have parroted Beijing's allegations. Malaysian and Indonesian leaders have agreed to continue their dialogues with Vietnam to insure peace and stability in Southeast Asia.[43]

In general, however, in the last half of 1980, a hard line prevailed in ASEAN in deference to Thailand. The five called on U.N. Secretary General Kurt Waldheim to station an observation team on the Thai-Cambodian border. Singaporean Prime Minister Lee Kwan Yew hinted that in light of the Vietnamese incursion, ASEAN should keep an "open mind" on whether the Association might become a military alliance in the future.[44]

One interesting feature of the varying perspectives ASEAN members brought to the Vietnamese military flare-up has been the Philippines' low profile. Manila may be cross-pressured on the issue. On the one hand it is strongly anticommunist and suspicious of all communist actors in the region. The Marcos government is confident, however, that it can cope with its internal communist insurgents without foreign assistance. Manila, therefore, resists entanglement in Thailand's problems, although for the sake of ASEAN solidarity it is willing to join Association condemnations of Vietnamese actions. Nevertheless, the Philippines does not want to become involved in either the Sino-Soviet or the Sino-Vietnamese conflicts—even indirectly through its ASEAN membership—and probably tacitly leans toward the Malaysian-Indonesian side on this issue.[45]

Concerned over the long-term political viability of the Khmer Rouge as the official Cambodian representative in the United Nations, in 1981 ASEAN leaders encouraged the formation of a new leadership for the resistance to replace the discredited Pol Pot group. This new anticommunist body, potentially composed of Prince Sihanouk's followers and various members of the anticommunist Khmer Serai under the prince's former prime minister, Son Sann, was a gambit quite different from the PRC-generated cosmetic replacement in 1980 of Pol Pot by Khieu Samphan as leader of the Khmer Rouge. Some ASEAN and American officials believed that if anticommunist Cambodians could transcend their own differences and effect a working relationship with the Khmer Rouge, the Heng Samrin regime could be kept out of the United Nations indefinitely. Then, a combination of Western economic aid to Vietnam and guarantees of Cambodian neutrality under Sihanouk or Son Sann would provide Hanoi with secure borders, permitting the Vietnamese to withdraw militarily and reduce their ties to the USSR.[46]

This scenario is much too sanguine, however. First, the anticommunist resistance groups are weak, divided, and lack significant military forces compared with the Khmer Rouge. Any integrated group—regardless of its nominal leaders—would in actuality be led by the Khmer Rouge. Second, Vietnam has doubled the size of its army since the Chinese invasion of 1979 and, with Soviet aid, can sustain forces in all three Indochinese countries. Even Vietnam's current economic crisis can be overcome since Hanoi can import rice from Cambodia as that country redevelops its fertile land.[47] Finally, while the Soviets will continue to drive a hard bargain with the Vietnamese, they will undoubtedly continue their aid because of the strategic advantages obtained through the use of Indochinese bases.

A meeting in Singapore among Sihanouk, Khieu Samphan, and Son Sann in August 1981 failed to reach an agreement to create a new coalition. China apparently decided not to press the Khmer Rouge to accept Son Sann's terms of complete political control of the resistance and exile to China of the top Khmer Rouge leaders.

ASEAN's persistent ambivalence toward a resolution of the Cambodian confrontation was manifest in behind-the-scenes differences at a July 1981 special U.N. conference on Cambodia. Although boycotted by the Soviet bloc and Indochina, more than two-thirds of U.N. members adopted a declaration once again appealing to Vietnam to withdraw its troops from Cambodia and endorsing the presence of a U.N. force during the pullout and the holding of free elections. The resolution essentially repeated earlier U.N. statements designed to sustain diplomatic pressure on Vietnam and buttress the Khmer resistance. Behind the facade of unity, however, lay important differences between ASEAN and China.

At bottom the ASEAN states wished to reassure Vietnam that Cambodia need not be a security concern. They initially proposed disarming all Cambodian factions following a Vietnamese withdrawal—a position strongly opposed by China and the Khmer Rouge since it would probably lead to a transfer of authority to some combination of Son Sann's Khmer People's National Liberation Front (KPNLF) and those supporting Prince Sihanouk. If a change of regime occurred in Cambodia, Beijing would lose its client, thus weakening its strategic position on Vietnam's western border. Even Singapore, which had taken the most adamant line against Hanoi of all ASEAN members, insisted that ASEAN was interested not in "bleeding" Vietnam but rather in reducing regional tension and diminishing the prospect of renewed violence.[48]

A political trap may lie hidden in the protracted negotiations among the Khmer Rouge, Sihanouk's supporters, and Son Sann's Khmer People's National Liberation Front (KPNLF). Should a united front be effected, then ASEAN must address the issue of supplying arms to a coalition government. If arms are openly supplied by ASEAN members to the resistance coalition, then ASEAN will for the first time challenge Vietnam militarily—albeit indirectly through arms aid to a counter-government. Interestingly, both the *Asian Wall Street Journal* (December 18, 1981) and the *Far Eastern Economic Review* (December 18, 1981) reported that the Thai military was unenthusiastic about this prospect. Arms supplies to Son Sann's forces would enhance the probability of internecine warfare between the Khmer Rouge and the KPNLF, rendering the Thai military's intermediary role more difficult, perhaps invite another pre-emptive border strike by the VPA, and generally permit Khmer resistance groups greater independence from Thai control. In sum, a militarily stronger resistance becomes a "wild card" that could further raise tensions between Vietnam and Thailand.

Thailand as the Front-line State

The area in general recognized that Thailand, of all the ASEAN states, would emphasize security matters, faced as it was with rebellion and subversion in and around its borders. In 1977, the Thai foreign minister stated his hopes that ASEAN partners would aid his country in the event of outside attack.[49] Indeed, insofar as ASEAN may develop a regional security role, its willingness to assist Thailand will be the bellwether. Thailand is ASEAN's front line with respect to security. The manner in which the Association assists Bangkok's efforts to maintain Thailand's territorial integrity should foretell whether the Association is willing to create a security program and what the nature of that program will be.

Thailand's current confrontation with Hanoi is a legacy that goes back centuries to periods of warring empires waxing and waning over Cambodia's territory.[50] More recently, the SRV's hostility toward and suspicion of Bangkok may be attributed to the latter's strong support for the American effort in the second Indochina war.

Thailand abandoned its fabled neutrality after 1954 because of its conviction that a divided Vietnam would be safer, especially if South Vietnam were an ally. If the United States succeeded in keeping China and the Soviet Union out of Southeast Asia, Thailand would have nothing to fear from a weak and divided Vietnam. For Thailand, two Vietnams were better than one.[51] Nevertheless, disagreements among Thai leaders over the amount of support to be given the American war effort grew throughout the 1960s as the possibility of a Vietnamese victory loomed ever larger. A growing nationalist mood within Thailand against its heavy dependence on U.S. military and economic largesse culminated in the student-led overthrow of the military regime in 1973.

Another irritant in Thai-Vietnamese relations was Thai and American policy toward Laos. Bangkok set out to build a Thai-oriented regime in Vientiane, in the hope of ultimately partitioning the country with Hanoi controlling the tribal hills and a lowland government leaning toward Thailand. The Thais would have established a buffer against Hanoi along the Mekong. (Lao attempts at neutralization during this period were weak efforts to protect their independence from both Thai and Vietnamese designs.)

In sum, Thailand's first choice was a weak divided Vietnam. Barring that, Bangkok worked toward a partition of Laos and the maintenance of a friendly Cambodia—under a U.S.-oriented Lon Nol after 1970—as territorial buffers against a strong Vietnam. By 1975, this Thai strategy had collapsed along with the hopes of its U.S. ally. Bangkok faced the worst of all possible outcomes: a hostile, powerful Vietnam bent on unifying Indochina and directly confronting Thailand along the whole of its vulnerable eastern border.

Moreover, Vietnam's victory in the second Indochina war loosed a new flood of refugees, adding to the thousands dating back to 1954 in northeastern Thailand. The refugees' demand to return to their homelands and determine their countries' political future was, in effect, a time bomb. Those who were hostile to the incumbent Indochinese governments gave Hanoi a pretext for accusing Bangkok of sheltering and creating an exile army. Those who supported Hanoi made Thailand fear a fifth-column movement and potential irredentism. Either way the Thais would lose. The refugees had created a Palestinian problem for Thailand that not only seemed intractable but actually grew with each new Vietnamese move against another ethnic or class group. Vietnamese persecution of resident Chinese, the bourgeoisie, and Laotian tribal minorities added to the exodus from Indochina. Many of the refugees moved west across the land frontiers into Thailand.

Despite its distaste for Pol Pot's Khmer Rouge after 1975 and periodic border clashes with that government over smuggling and the presence of anticommunist Cambodian refugees in Thailand, Bangkok was generally prepared to accommodate Cambodia because at bottom Pol Pot's forces were anti-Vietnamese. Thailand was even prepared to tolerate Laotian and Cambodian support of the CPT during this period.

By 1978 the Khmer Rouge government, deeply concerned over Vietnamese encroachments in its eastern provinces, called on Thailand for diplomatic assistance, pointing out that ASEAN had a stake in maintaining an independent Cambodia.[52] The Khmer Rouge argument fit long-term Thai strategy nicely; Bangkok not only began to tilt toward Phnom Penh but also moved to improve relations with Cambodia's major backer—the PRC. A number of benefits followed. China seemed to reduce its assistance to Thai insurgents, while stepping up its economic aid for Thailand, including much-needed petroleum. Reports of more grisly Thai cooperation with the Khmer Rouge also surfaced in 1978. Refugees told an American columnist that in the last half of 1977 and early 1978, Thai border police, hoping to stem the flow of Cambodians into Thailand, either turned away or shot most of those attempting to cross.[53] Indeed, during this period the number of refugees added to Thai camps fell precipitously.

When, however, Vietnamese forces crossed en masse into Cambodia, Thailand once again appeared to have backed the losing side in Indochina. Bangkok's initial reaction was to declare its neutrality, insisting that the government would permit no activities on the Thai side of the border threatening to any Cambodian government, regardless of its political composition. At first Hanoi, too, seemed conciliatory, emphasizing the advantages to Thailand of a new government that would bring "military provocations against Thailand . . . to an end."[54]

SRV hopes for Thai neutrality were soon dashed, however, as the Thai military facilitated the movement of Chinese arms (through Sino-Thai arms brokers) to Khmer Rouge guerrillas just across the border in the Cardamon mountains. The introduction of VPA forces into this area inevitably led to a deterioration in Bangkok's relations with Hanoi. In an effort to justify its military occupation of Laos and Cambodia as well as its decision to expel ethnic Chinese from Indochina, Hanoi charged the PRC with infiltrating hostile Chinese into northern Vietnam, with training and supplying the Khmer Rouge in Thai sanctuaries, and with similarly organizing and equipping "Lao traitors" in Yunnan province for subversion. In the face of these challenges, said Hanoi radio, "it is natural that the peoples of the three countries of the Indochinese Peninsula . . . are helping one another to oppose hegemonistic and expansionist acts, and this is compatible with the UN Charter."[55]

By hugging the Thai border during the dry season, the Khmer Rouge hoped to constrain Vietnamese search-and-destroy operations since the VPA would avoid shooting into Thai territory. Moreover, Thailand permitted belligerents from both sides to escape into Thailand so long as they returned to Cambodia in a reasonably short time. This policy of safe conduct amounted to sanctuary for Pol Pot's forces and provided them access to supplies.[56]

ASEAN provided Thailand with strong diplomatic support. In addition to the association's U.N. resolution urging Hanoi to withdraw its forces from Cambodia, the late June 1979 Bali Foreign Ministers' Conference warned that any incursion into Thailand would affect the security of all five ASEAN members. As usual, Singapore's position was the most extreme. It insisted that any attack on Thailand was an attack on ASEAN. More significant, perhaps, was the statement of Malaysian Deputy Prime Minister Mahatir Mohammed that if Thailand's security were threatened, Malaysia, Indonesia, and Thailand had a military "understanding" that could be activated to assist Bangkok. He did not reveal the nature of this "understanding," however.[57] Indonesia, in contrast, seemed much less enthusiastic; Foreign Minister Mochtar reiterated that Jakarta did not consider Vietnam an enemy.[58]

Thailand, too, had no desire for a direct confrontation. Asked about Vietnamese forays into Thai territory, Prime Minister Kriangsak minimized their significance: "We may know where the border is, but others may stray across it because they do not know. In any event, it must be pointed out that the intruders are not necessarily Vietnamese soldiers, but could be soldiers loyal to any side. We must not make it sound as if we are an enemy of Vietnam." Nevertheless, Kriangsak expressed interest in a possible meeting of ASEAN defense ministers so long as it did not formalize military ties on an ASEAN-wide basis but merely led to an exchange of information.[59] Reports have circulated of some informal military assistance to Thailand, including the presence of Indonesian intelligence specialists with the Thai military on Thailand's northeastern border.[60]

Thai analysts themselves are not sanguine about the Association's ability to assist militarily in the event of a serious Vietnamese challenge. ASEAN states could help financially to defray the heavy costs of a long-term military confrontation, but as far as military action is concerned, Thailand sees China as a much more credible tacit ally and a more potent deterrent to Hanoi.[61] Nevertheless, inflation-fueled economic instability brought on by disproportionate military expenditures may be more of a threat to the Thai government over the long run than is the VPA.

In late 1979, Thailand released a report from a U.N. fact-finding team estimating that over 500,000 Cambodians were massing near the Thai border both to obtain food and to flee into Thailand should the fighting become too intense. Thai authorities also claimed to have captured 300 Vietnamese troops who had crossed into the country on surveillance and intelligence missions.[62]

Heng Samrin's foreign minister, Hun Sen, admitted that Vietnam could not wipe out the Khmer Rouge without crossing into Thailand and eliminating their base camps. He went on to say that Hanoi was not prepared to do this, for it could lead to renewed fighting with China and the possibility of American intervention.[63] As if to reinforce this interpretation, PRC Foreign Minister Huang Hua, on a visit to Bangkok, pledged massive arms aid to the Khmer Rouge as the only way to force the Vietnamese to leave Cambodia. Indonesian media—ever suspicious of China—pointed out that Huang Hua's decision to make this announcement in Thailand was designed to suggest Thai complicity and incite Hanoi to further animosity.[64]

The new Thai prime minister, General Prem Tinsulanond, however, promised General Suharto that Thailand would not permit China to use Thai territory for any massive supply of arms to the Khmer Rouge. This position served to reassure both Indonesian and Malaysian leaders (the authors of the Kuantan statement) that Bangkok had not opted for Beijing, thus undermining ASEAN neutrality.[65] Further underlying the Indonesian-Malaysian position is a preference for a Hanoi-dominated Indochina—if a Vietnamese withdrawal from Cambodia cannot be effected—as opposed to renewed Chinese influence in the region through the Khmer Rouge. Thailand, however, probably holds the opposite preference. That is the crux of ASEAN's dilemma with respect to Cambodia: how to maintain ASEAN solidarity and simultaneously satisfy the perceived security needs of at least three members who see different primary adversaries.

Thailand's "humanitarian" assistance to the Cambodian refugees encamped along the border is also complicated by the refugees' political fractionalization. Periodic firefights among Cambodian factions for control of the refugees have led Thai military authorities to cut off aid to the camps from time to time. While much of the fighting occurs between Khmer Rouge and anticommunist refugee groups, a good deal of it is little more than shootouts among bandits vying for control of the lucrative international relief trade both in the refugee camps and across the border in Cambodia.

In early June 1980 a new, ominous tone appeared in Vietnamese and Heng Samrin propaganda toward Thailand. The Phnom Penh news agency warned: "Thai territory has been used as a base for training and supplying . . . criminals. Permanent tension prevails along the frontier, threatening the SRV's security . . . [The Kampuchean People's Revolutionary Council] cannot allow anyone to interfere in its internal affairs or violate its security and territorial integrity."[66] Hanoi and Phnom Penh were becoming increasingly frustrated over the VPA's inability to eliminate the Khmer Rouge guerrillas and attributed their viability to Thai sanctuary and assistance. If the latter could be cut off, Vietnam calculated, the Khmer Rouge would atrophy.

On June 10, the Thai government announced that it had decided to allow any of the 175,000 Khmer residing in Thailand who so desired to return to Cambodia. From Phnom Penh's perspective, this appeared to be a recruitment device for the Khmer Rouge and potentially could change the whole balance of the guerrilla war. Both Hanoi and Phnom Penh warned there would be retribution.[67] Between June 23 and 25, VPA forces crossed the frontier and overran two large encampments, temporarily seized two Thai border villages, and shelled others. Interrogation of captured Vietnamese soldiers revealed that only about two companies of Vietnamese troops were involved in the three-day operation. The Vietnamese attacked only after some 5,000 refugees had been repatriated over a week-long period.[68]

Once again, the Vietnamese became the target of international political opprobrium. Singaporean Deputy Prime Minister Sinnathamby Rajaratnam called the incident "another illustration which shows that the Vietnamese cannot be believed. They said they would not cross into Thailand." The ASEAN foreign ministers, meeting in Kuala Lumpur, denounced "this irresponsible and dangerous act," warning that it presented "a grave and direct threat to the security of Thailand and the Southeast Asian region."[69]

Despite the harsh rhetoric of the ASEAN statement, which condemned Vietnam by name for the first time, the Association announced no new security arrangements. Moreover, Hanoi's incursion into Thailand, though clearly establishing a new and more dangerous limit in the conflict, was conducted for specific and limited purposes: (1) to break up two major refugee camps and force their occupants deeper into the Thai interior; (2) to signal to Thailand that the refugee camps could not be used as Khmer Rouge recruiting centers—at least not in tandem with large-scale Thai repatriation; and (3) to reduce and, if possible, halt the distribution of international aid at the frontier, which fed a major black market operation in Cambodia and drew peasants away from their fields. One question was left unanswered: Hanoi's willingness to permit the continued existence of refugee camps straddling the border on the basis of the status quo ante; that is, no large-scale Thai repatriation even though low-level anti-Vietnam activities would continue to emanate from the camps.

While Indonesia and Malaysia agreed to join Thailand's harsh condemnation of Vietnam over the June border incursion, it is clear that both had reservations. These new developments set back prospects for the political settlement Kuala Lumpur and Jakarta prefer—recognition of Indochina as a Vietnamese sphere of influence with the provision that VPA forces not be located near the Thai border. These two ASEAN members emphatically oppose exacerbation of Thai-Vietnamese tensions since they encourage China to play an even larger role as Thailand's tacit ally, push other ASEAN states away from neutrality, and appear to legitimate a security role for Beijing in Southeast Asia.

Vietnam, in turn, sees Thailand as the main obstacle to ASEAN's acceptance of the status quo in Cambodia. Hanoi's decision to disperse the refugees away from the border by military force cost Vietnam in its relations with ASEAN. Vietnam chose to pay this diplomatic price in order to cut off a source of new manpower for the anti-Vietnam/anti-Heng Samrin guerrillas and to close the land bridge that supplied them. One benefit has been to reduce temporarily the black market in relief goods, which had corrupted Vietnamese forces and disrupted agricultural activities in western Cambodia.

Vietnam has deliberately downplayed the border incursion incident, assuring ASEAN that it did not represent an initial movement toward war with Thailand. By insisting that Vietnamese forces did not cross the Thai border (though, in fact, they did) and that border tensions are really only a product of the "Beijing expansionists" in collaboration with a group of "far right Thai reactionaries" the SRV can still urge ASEAN—including Thailand—to continue searching for a modus vivendi with the Indochinese governments.

Nevertheless, the SRV has once again flexed its military muscles, demonstrating that Thailand is no match for it and that the VPA will sustain operations all along the Thai border as long as Bangkok continues to provide sanctuary for Cambodian refugees. The key question is, Will these tactics cow Thailand into acquiescence or, rather, will they serve to move ASEAN states closer to a common security position with Chinese and American aid? If the latter, then Vietnam's tactics will have proven counterproductive.

4 | EXTERNAL GUARANTEES AND INTERNAL SOLIDARITY

For an organization ostensibly committed to the promotion of its members' nonalignment, ASEAN devotes much time to determining who its external guarantors might be as well as how to cope with current and future adversaries. The convergence of Sino-Soviet, Sino-Vietnamese, and—increasingly—Soviet-American competition in Southeast Asia has, at the least, postponed ASEAN's hopes for the creation of ZOPFAN to the distant future. The Association's plans for economic development through cooperation must now go hand-in-hand with security consultations, joint diplomatic efforts to protect territorial integrity, and growing military collaboration. Originally, none of these was to have become an integral part of the Association's activities. Particularly since the Vietnamese invasion of Cambodia in January 1979, they have dominated ASEAN's agenda.

This chapter examines the ASEAN states' views of the roles that friendly great powers—particularly the United States and Japan—might play in the security of the region; ASEAN concerns over long-term Soviet and Vietnamese designs; and finally the ability of the Association to adhere to nonalignment in an environment that appears to be moving toward a new polarization in the 1980s—this time between competitive communist centers.

ASEAN and the United States

In all ASEAN states the United States is a major investor and trader, and each state has a significant resident American business community. The United States sells military equipment on easy terms to the five, has a security treaty with the Philippines, and an executive understanding going back almost twenty years with Thailand, pledging assistance in the event of communist aggression.

America has supported ASEAN strongly, seeing it as the best hope for stability in Southeast Asia. As a major investor, Washington is comfortable with regimes such as those in ASEAN—oriented toward international trade and investment and an international market economy. Relations with ASEAN states have not been entirely free from care, however. Growing nationalist sentiment in ASEAN academic and business communities has led to resentment over the extent of economic control exercised by foreign MNCs. On the other side, U.S. civil rights activists within the Carter administration were exercised over the authoritarianism characteristic to some degree of all ASEAN regimes. Arbitrary arrest and detention of political opponents annually drew opprobrium from congressional investigators in mandated State Department human rights reports. Nevertheless, there is room for optimism about these states because, as Bruce Grant observes, there is

> a genuine intention to improve living standards, absence of official terror and brutality, relatively open education with a concern for scholarship, freedom of citizens to travel abroad and receive information from . . . non-government sponsored [media] and other sources of authority in the community. A society which allows its citizens these kinds of freedoms is likely to turn more to the United States and the industrial democracies than to the Soviet Union, the People's Republic of China or the Socialist Republic of Vietnam.[1]

While the United States remained involved militarily on mainland Southeast Asia in the 1950s and 1960s, Thailand—as the front-line anticommunist state—felt relatively secure. It could risk a degree of belligerence toward the communist movements in Indochina as well as toward their Chinese and Russian backers. The problem arose in the next decade when the United States re-evaluated the importance of the region to American security. Suddenly, the Americans viewed as peripheral areas the Thais considered vital. Moreover, Thailand faced the prospect of rapidly generating a new set of diplomatic arrangements to insure its security that would mollify recent adversaries while still maintaining Thai territorial integrity.

Interestingly, Thailand's archipelagic partners in ASEAN did not necessarily share its concern over the American withdrawal at the end of the second Indochina war. The Philippines still had an active security treaty with the United States as well as American bases. Indonesian leaders discounted the American withdrawal from mainland Southeast Asia because they believed Washington would maintain the Seventh Fleet in the western Pacific at sufficient strength to deter any threat to them. The consensus among defense analysts in these countries was that the United States was shifting to a "blue water defence which would encompass the Philippines and Indonesia."[2]

The Philippine military, a particularly important political group after martial law was declared in 1972, was committed to maintaining the American connection. Military assistance from the United States averaged $30 million annually between 1972 and 1976 and grew another 25 percent in 1977, accounting for between 10 and 20 percent of the country's total military budget annually from 1972 to 1978.[3] These transfers were essential to the government's suppression of the Moro Rebellion and continued action against the NPA in other parts of the islands.

Nevertheless, Marcos was skeptical of the utility of the Mutual Security Treaty with the United States and anxious about the vagueness of the provisions dealing with the treaty's coverage. The Philippines was concerned not over outright conventional attack but rather over whether the treaty could be invoked in smaller armed conflicts growing out of Manila's conflicting territorial claims with other states.[4] In the late 1960s, for example, Manila wanted to invoke the treaty to cover local skirmishes emanating from the Sabah dispute. More recently, Marcos raised questions about its applicability to the Spratly Islands issue. The United States demurred from becoming involved in these disputes, of course, insisting that they were matters for negotiation and international law rather than military force. Moreover, it is unlikely that Marcos expected any statement of U.S. support for his claims. Rather, he was making a case for compensation when the U.S. base arrangements came up for renegotiation in the late 1970s. In effect he argued that because the bases were valueless in terms of possible Philippine conflicts, Manila should be reimbursed for their continued operation.

In the early 1980s, the Philippines began to display some interest in air and coastal defense. Probably in response to the growing Soviet presence around the disputed Spratly Islands, Philippine forces are now garrisoned in the area; and Manila is purchasing Fokker-27 naval surveillance aircraft. Renewed American assurances to the Philippines are inherent in the U.S. Navy's 1981 decision to base a Seventh Fleet missile cruiser at Subic Bay.[5]

In sum, from the mid-1970s, ASEAN views of the nature, importance, and interests covered by U.S. security arrangements in Southeast Asia varied widely. No one wished to see the United States leave precipitously, but there was little consensus over the necessity of maintaining American military power in the region.

Beginning in 1978, some three years after the Indochina debacle, the United States began to rebuild its military profile in East Asia. From 1973 to 1977 Seventh Fleet strength had declined from three carriers and 29 surface combat ships to two carriers and 18 surface ships, while the Soviet Pacific Fleet was moving in the other direction. These opposing trends led Japan's Defense Agency vice-minister, Ko Maruyama, to warn that the United States had only a "limited" capability to defend East Asian sea-lanes against the Russians. At the same time, Admiral Elmo Zumwalt declared that the decline in American naval strength could mean that in the event of a global crisis America would have to abandon its Pacific allies in order to defend the continental United States and Persian Gulf region.[6]

If the United States withdrew from an East Asian defense position, reinvolvement would be a slow process. Military officials point out that it would take seventeen days for a carrier task force to steam from the west coast to the Indian Ocean. Moreover, with only 140,000 military personnel deployed forward of Guam in 1979, the United States was maintaining its lowest force level in East Asia since before World War II.[7]

While military capabilities declined in the latter 1970s, America's commercial interests boomed. By 1978, trade with the Asian-Pacific countries exceeded trade with Europe. The investment return for the region of approximately 15 percent exceeded the return on U.S. European investment by 3 percentage points.[8]

In February 1978, U.S. Defense Secretary Harold Brown revealed a five-year military development plan that would upgrade the U.S. military capability in the region. By 1983, Brown claimed, Trident and cruise missiles would be deployed with the Seventh Fleet along with F-14 fighters for the carriers and F-15s for the Air Force. The Pacific fleet would be rebuilt to a strength of six carriers, 80 surface combat ships, and 32 submarines.

Brown's plans for increased U.S. air and naval strength could be interpreted as a new variation on the Guam Doctrine, which had guided U.S. security policy in East Asia in the wake of the Indochina war. While the Guam Doctrine stated that the United States could not be expected to commit ground forces to assist an Asian ally against external aggression, it tacitly implied that air and naval power could be brought to bear in a variety of ways: (1) to interdict the aggressor, (2) to attack aggressor forces directly, and (3) to provide supplies to friendly governments.

Little of this modernization had occurred, however, when Vietnam marched into Cambodia in early 1979 and China launched its counterstrike on the northern Vietnamese border. After the Soviet invasion of Afghanistan and the seizure of U.S. hostages in Iran, Asian analysts began to wonder whether U.S. military capability was a useless resource. As one political scientist from the University of Singapore put it:

> For the ASEAN countries, the conclusion is clear. First, the possibility of an active military presence by the United States can be discounted. The American leadership has not been shown to be extremely positive to other crises such as the hostage issue in Teheran or the current invasion of Afghanistan by the Soviet troops. The best the ASEAN countries can hope for would be exhortations, the mobilization of world opinion and an increase in military aid and credit sales.[9]

Asian leaders fear that if the United States perceives its interests in the region to be tertiary, American incentives to accept the costs and risks of military intervention in the event of Vietnamese (or Russian) aggression will be low. Consider, for example, the not unlikely prospect of the USSR's providing the Vietnamese navy with precision guided missiles sometime in the 1980s. These weapons could endanger the Seventh Fleet in the event of a maritime confrontation. Would the United States risk such destruction to intervene in a regional conflict or would it choose to remain uninvolved? The answer is not apparent, and this worries Washington's Asian allies.

ASEAN also saw normalization of relations between the United States and the PRC in January 1979 as a mixed blessing. For the Philippines, the new relationship signified the return to "a real balance of power in Asia." President Marcos observed that by establishing a three-way link among Tokyo, Beijing, and Washington, "the United States reestablishes itself as an Asian and Pacific power."[10] The ASEAN states suspicious of Beijing, however, may not be so sanguine about the prospects of a security relationship between the United States and China. The stronger that relationship, the greater their reluctance to seek U.S. support for fear of providing opportunities for Chinese intervention as well. It must be remembered that although ASEAN has uniformly condemned Vietnam for the boat people refugees, most of them are ethnic Chinese. This serves the SRV's strategic purpose by clouding the issue of Vietnamese aggression and creating strains within ASEAN over PRC intentions toward the thousands of new Chinese residents in Malaysia and, to a lesser extent, Indonesia and the Philippines.

Perhaps the best prospect for continued American security involvement in Southeast Asia derives from developments in the Middle East and South Asia. The importance of maintaining open sea-lanes for Persian Gulf oil, the potentially enhanced Soviet threat to that region resulting from the Russian occupation of Afghanistan, and the establishment of a viscerally anti-American Islamic fundamentalist regime in Iran virtually compel an increase in the U.S. military presence in that region. Since 1979, there has been talk of a U.S. Indian Ocean fleet; the continued improvement of Diego Garcia atoll as a U.S. naval station as well as the suspension of talks between Washington and Moscow on demilitarization of the Indian Ocean should be understood in terms of these U.S. perceptions.

The United States could respond to tension in Southwest Asia either by creating a separate Indian Ocean fleet or enhancing the strength of the Seventh Fleet. The choice is not as important to ASEAN as the belief that the United States remains committed to maintaining freedom of the seas, including the Malacca Strait. Concurrent with Washington's decision to maintain naval forces permanently in the Persian Gulf–Indian Ocean region have come expressions of commitment to the ASEAN countries. Secretary of State Cyrus Vance, at the conclusion of the July 1979 ASEAN Foreign Ministers' Conference in Bali, reaffirmed the United States' moral and treaty obligations to help ASEAN countries maintain their independence and territorial integrity. In order to fulfill these commitments, Washington would, Vance promised, increase and speed up military assistance to individual ASEAN states and undertake to enhance American military capabilities in Asia, the Pacific, and the Indian Ocean.[11] Secretary of State Haig reiterated these assurances at a June 1981 ASEAN foreign ministers' meeting, promising military assistance to the five on easy terms.

Assistant Secretary of State Richard Holbrooke was even more emphatic: the United States viewed Thailand as the key to ASEAN and ASEAN as the key to Southeast Asia. The United States had to demonstrate its support for Thailand as evidence of its good intentions toward the region. A limited manifestation of this support was the 1979 American pledge of $40 million worth of military equipment. Moreover, Holbrooke pointed out, no Vietnamese military action can occur outside its borders without Soviet aid and presumably approval since, although Vietnam has a powerful army, its economy is straitened and its logistics entirely dependent on the USSR.[12] Therefore, Vietnamese ambitions could be somewhat constrained by Soviet-American understand-ings over the nature of their competition in the Third World. If the Russians desired to improve relations with ASEAN and Japan, presum-ably they would work to restrain Vietnam's military actions along the Thai border. On the other hand, if the Soviets view ASEAN as dis-united and vacillating, Japan as indifferent, and the United States as un-willing to become involved in a limited Asian conflict, the USSR might agree to a more aggressive Vietnamese posture toward Thailand, partic-ularly if Hanoi sweetened the pot by offering the USSR full-scale base rights at Camranh Bay and Da Nang.

The Sino-American entente reached new heights with the visit of Secretary of Defense Harold Brown to Beijing in January 1980. Speaking at the farewell banquet, Brown averred that Chinese and American "strategic interests converge in many instances" and that "our parallel actions will be mutually reinforcing." Brown pointed to the common assessment of the Soviet-backed Vietnamese threat to Southeast Asia and stated "the task before us is to insure that our converging assess-ments are translated into effective responses."[13] According to a New York Times report, Brown also stated that the United States would wel-come Chinese military assistance if VPA forces crossed into Thailand.[14]

In seeming response to these expressions of Sino-American coopera-tion, the foreign ministers of the three Indochinese countries stated in a January communiqué that the Vietnamese overthrow of Pol Pot demon-strated the PRC's weakness as did the lack of an American response at the time.[15] In short, ASEAN should not rely on a weak Sino-American "alliance" for protection, for neither country could do much to help ASEAN members. Indeed, some ASEAN publicists have expressed res-ervations over American support for their military buildups. An Indone-sian writer, noting Holbrooke's support for Jakarta's military moderniza-tion program, stated that it would be better for Indonesia to finance the program through domestic resources than to accept U.S. aid and appear to be beholden to U.S. interests.[16] His apparent concern was that the Indonesian military not be seen as an anti-Vietnamese or anti-Soviet force.

Even Thailand, though tacitly facilitating Chinese aid to the Khmer Rouge by permitting the transit of Chinese goods through Thai terri-tory, has publicly affected a neutral posture. Chinese leaders have urged Thailand to join the anti-Vietnamese cause openly, and the PRC has provided inducements to do so, such as the "friendship" option for badly needed crude oil. Nevertheless, Bangkok has preferred to keep its op-tions open; for example, it signed a baht 1 million (U.S. $50,000) export credit for Vietnam in January 1980.

Despite growing Sino-American cooperation vis-à-vis the Soviet Union, the policies of the two powers have not converged with respect to Cambodian developments and the future of Southeast Asia. The PRC doggedly adheres to the discredited Khmer Rouge and insists that the Vietnamese invasion of Cambodia and the Soviet occupation of Afghanistan are not local incidents but part of a Russian-directed global strategy to gain control of the world's oil routes and establish the geographic dominance necessary to obstruct Asian commerce. The United States, on the other hand, still offers normalization and economic assistance to Hanoi on the condition that it demonstrate a willingness to cooperate with America, ASEAN, and Japan—presumably by working out an arrangement for military withdrawal from Cambodia.[17]

Vietnamese acceptance of the Indonesian-Malaysian Kuantan principle could be an initial move in this direction, for it would allow Vietnam to develop a cooperative relationship with ASEAN while maintaining a dominant role in Indochina, so long as it agreed to withdraw its forces first from the Thai border region and then from Cambodia in a "reasonable" period of time. Such an agreement would give Hanoi the necessary latitude to reduce its dependence on Moscow and subsequently diminish its confrontation with China since the latter is to a large extent a function of the Soviet-Vietnamese alliance. The problem with this optimistic scenario, however, is that Washington is simply not as credible a guarantor against China as Moscow is. The more closely the United States and the PRC are linked politically, the less likely Vietnam will look to America for assistance.

President Carter's spring 1980 reversal of a 1977 defense decision should enhance America's credibility as a Pacific power over time. In 1977, as a result of budgetary constraints, Carter announced a "swing strategy" of meeting NATO's needs in a crisis by moving Seventh or Third Fleet units to Europe. By 1980, with the situation altered in West Asia and the Soviet-Vietnamese alliance, Carter reversed himself, insisting that defense of the oil lanes from the Persian Gulf to East Asia was vital to all noncommunist states, including the members of NATO. The actual buildup of naval capability would take several years, however.

As the commander-in-chief of the Pacific Command, Admiral Maurice Wiesner, explained to Congress in 1979: "Our fundamental geopolitical, economic, and military situation has changed in the Pacific-Asia region. Japan is now our leading overseas trading partner. Our primary adversary in Asia is now the Soviet Union, and the balance of naval forces in the Pacific Command has changed markedly."[18] The contrast with 1977 could not be more dramatic. At that time the United States was seeking to demilitarize the Indian Ocean. Now it is in the process of deploying a substantial naval force in the Indian Ocean, seeking base rights in Somalia, Kenya, and Oman, and creating an airborne rapid deployment force. These developments not only emphasize Asia but more particularly the southern part of Asia—shifting at least some of the Pacific Command's emphasis away from the north Pacific.

The first test of U.S. resolve in this new Pacific-oriented situation was its reaction to Vietnam's limited, three-day incursion into Thailand. As proof of the United States' commitment to Thai integrity and ASEAN security, President Carter ordered an immediate airlift of small arms, artillery, ammunition, and an improved version of the old U.S. Patton tank. The United States paid for the cost of the airlift, but Thailand paid for the arms. The exercise was essentially symbolic, designed to impress pro-Western countries in Asia with the administration's determination to respond quickly to Soviet-supported military aggression. The military significance of the arms delivered was minimal. Thailand's total military establishment of 216,000 is no match for Vietnam's 200,000 battle-hardened forces deployed in Laos and Cambodia and backed by nearly one million more in the SRV.

Nevertheless, Washington is increasing military aid to Thailand, from $40 million in 1979 to a projected $80 million for fiscal 1982.[19] Carter ordered a new assault force of 1,800 marines complete with artillery, tanks, antitank units, and support troops into the Indian Ocean.[20] This force could be used either in Southwest or Southeast Asia. However, if Hanoi, with one of the largest standing armies in the world and 1,500 tanks, decided upon a major invasion of Thailand, the only effective American response would probably be air strikes from Okinawa, Clark Air Base, and carriers in the Seventh Fleet. American troops in South Korea and Okinawa are insufficient to repel a full-scale Vietnamese invasion.

ASEAN and Japan

While ASEAN increasingly desires a substantial U.S. military presence in Southeast Asia to balance the Soviet-Vietnamese alliance (and, in the future, a Chinese force projection capability), the Association is also concerned about the activities of another "friendly" state—Japan. During the 1970s considerable debate occurred throughout East Asia over whether Japan could play a role in Southeast Asian security and the kind of role it might be. For the most part Japan abjures military activities, citing Article IX of its constitution (although usually interpreted as precluding the movement of Japanese forces beyond the home islands, this proscription has been violated on several occasions as ships from the Maritime Self-Defense Force have conducted maneuvers with the Seventh Fleet and other friendly navies in Southeast Asia and the mid-Pacific).

Most discussion of Japan's security role emphasizes economic rather than military possibilities. Some argue that there should be a division of labor between the United States and Japan. Washington would provide the military umbrella for the region, while Japan would increase its economic aid, trade, and investment. Arguments against this arrangement include (1) the fear that animosity toward Japan's already dominant economic role in Southeast Asia would rub off on the United States if it appeared to be supporting Japan's domination; (2) U.S. aid to Southeast Asia would be reduced since the region would be considered the primary economic responsibility of Japan; and (3) U.S. business would be put at a disadvantage since with Japanese economic predominance would come Japanese government-subsidized loans.

In fact, Japan's dominant position in Southeast Asian trade was an established fact by 1980.[21] In 1978, trade with Southeast Asia reached almost $30 billion, or about 17 percent of Japan's global trade. This figure equals about 80 percent of U.S.-Japan trade and almost half that between Japan and the EEC. Indonesia, Malaysia, and Brunei provide just under 26 percent of Japan's petroleum imports. For almost two decades Japan has been the first or second leading trading partner of every country in the region. (See Table 17.)

Japan's foreign aid program in Southeast Asia has been notoriously self-serving. More than any other developed state's aid, Japan's is in the form of loans and "tied aid" rather than open grants. Seventy-five percent of Japanese aid involves credits for commercial purposes, primarily from three sources: (1) the Import-Export Bank of Japan, which is explicitly committed to promoting Japanese commerce; (2) the Overseas Economic Cooperation Fund, which provides intergovernmental loans on terms easier than those of the Import-Export Bank; and (3) private commercial banks. The first and third are expressly designed to promote Japan's commercial well-being.

A similar picture emerges with investments. Over 25 percent of the country's direct overseas investments in 1977 ($5.6 billion) was concentrated in Southeast Asia. This figure slightly exceeded Japan's investments in the United States for the same period. Significantly, $4 billion of this total had been invested after 1973.

In light of these figures, Prime Minister Fukuda's 1977 promise to ASEAN to provide U.S. $1 billion toward Association industrial projects (pending feasibility studies and their designation as ASEAN projects) seems less a breakthrough in altruism than a restatement of old themes.

Presumably, the Japanese loan would be tied once again to the purchase of Japanese goods and services. Moreover, the ASEAN states are skeptical of Japanese political priorities in Asia. Within one year after Fukuda's pledge, Japan signed a friendship treaty with China that facilitated multimillion-dollar credit arrangements for a host of PRC industrial projects. ASEAN leaders believe that China, in effect, has become a favored rival for scarce Japanese capital, both because Japan sees the political relationship between Tokyo and Beijing as more important and also because Japanese industrialists envision an economic axis combining Japanese technology with talented Chinese manpower.[22]

Despite China's inability to honor orders for over $3 billion in Japanese plant and equipment in 1981, Japanese businessmen agreed to discuss ways of refinancing the loans. ASEAN observers noted sourly to this author in spring 1981 that not only would Japan refuse to consider such concessional terms for ASEAN projects but also that none of the loans for ASEAN industries had yet been approved four years after Fukuda initially proposed them. Only Indonesia's fertilizer project had progressed to the stage of a feasibility study. Indeed, under Prime Minister Suzuki Zenko, the Japanese government has adopted an entirely new economic orientation toward ASEAN, downplaying industrial showcase projects and offering support instead for educational and agricultural development.

TABLE 17

JAPAN–SOUTHEAST ASIAN TRADE, 1978
(millions of U.S. dollars)

	Exports	Imports	Total	Trade Balance	Rank of Japan in Nation's Total Trade
Brunei	51	1,403	1,454	−1,352	1
Burma	232	51	283	181	1
Hong Kong	3,112	501	3,613	2,611	2
Indonesia	2,114	5,284	7,398	−3,170	1
Malaysia	1,168	1,911	3,079	−743	1
Philippines	1,559	1,066	2,625	493	1
Singapore	2,345	878	3,223	1,467	1
Taiwan	3,615	1,764	5,379	1,851	2
Thailand	1,541	849	2,390	692	1
Vietnam	218	51	269	167	1
	15,955	13,758	29,713	+2,197	

SOURCE: International Monetary Fund, *Direction of Trade Yearbook, 1979*.

Nevertheless, Southeast Asia's integration into the Japanese economy has become too well established for China to cut into it significantly. By imaginatively using supplier credits to expand the region's capacity for providing raw materials, semiprocessed goods, and labor-intensive products for Japan's economy, Tokyo has created an interdependent relationship that promises to continue for some time. The relationship is cemented by the Japanese practice of accepting repayment of supplier credits in shipments of the materials produced.

ASEAN has attempted to convince Japan to support a raw-material export price stabilization scheme (STABEX) that would protect a number of the Association's commodities from the vagaries of the export market. Japanese agreement, some analysts argue, would be a sign of ASEAN's importance and an earnest of Japan's commitment to the region's economic stability. STABEX would also be easier for Japan to implement than would ASEAN's other main request—reduction in tariff and nontariff barriers to ASEAN products, which, the Association claims, account for the bilateral trade deficits accumulated by Thailand, Singapore, and the Philippines.

Although Japan has been somewhat less than accommodating on trade and investment complaints emanating from ASEAN, Tokyo has increasingly deferred to the five on matters of security importance in Southeast Asia—perhaps following the American lead. For example, after Vietnam's occupation of Cambodia in early 1979, Japanese Prime Minister Ohira Masayoshi told Deng Xiaoping that Japan's policy toward Cambodia would be decided only after "close consultation" with ASEAN.[23] Similarly, after China launched its punitive incursion into northern Vietnam, Japanese Foreign Minister Sonoda Sunao visited Indonesia to coordinate Tokyo's stand with ASEAN's. Tokyo backed ASEAN's condemnation of Vietnam both by continuing to recognize the defeated Khmer Rouge diplomatically and by freezing economic aid to the SRV, but directed no such sanctions against China for its attack.[24]

Japan also increased its aid to Thailand and Indonesia in 1980, including a record 57 billion yen (U.S. $270 million) for Thailand, up from the 47 billion yen ($220 million) of the previous year. Seven billion of the amount was a free grant. Indonesia was promised over 61 billion yen ($290 million), up from 50 billion ($240 million) in 1979. In both cases Tokyo explained the increases as part of a policy of concentrating economic assistance on those countries near troubled areas of the world.[25]

The author's own interviews in ASEAN capitals in 1979 and 1981 revealed a growing perception of the Association's importance to Japan and a belief that, like it or not, the region would see a growing Japanese maritime *military* presence in Southeast Asia in the 1980s. ASEAN military officials expected to see joint U.S.-Japanese naval patrols, perhaps in cooperation with Australia. Officials in the Philippine Ministry of Foreign Affairs indicated no apprehension about such developments "as long as they are in conjunction with the United States and limited to maintaining open sea-lanes."[26]

While observers viewed a growing Japanese security role in Southeast Asia as almost inevitable during the 1980s, they remained vaguely concerned about its implications. A possible repetition of the World War II experience was not a fear. Rather, a question raised on several occasions expressed concern over the new combination of Japan as the region's dominant economic power and as a military power in the region. What kind of political leverage could a weak ASEAN exercise over such a Japan? Related to this apprehension was the fear that if Japan increased its military strength in Southeast Asia, the United States would be tempted to reduce the size of the Seventh Fleet and transfer those military resources elsewhere.

Subsequent interviews among Japanese defense theorists reinforced some ASEAN views. The consensus among those interviewed was that it was unlikely ASEAN could become a regional security organization. Therefore, responsibility for the maintenance of open sea-lanes would fall primarily on the Seventh Fleet, perhaps with a Japanese contingent.

One thoughtful observer outlined the possible conditions that might make Japan undertake a greater regional defense role.[27] First, there would have to be significant new pressures from the international environment, such as an increased Soviet military presence in the region. Second, the Japan Self-Defense Forces would have to modernize their air and naval capabilities by buying new U.S. systems. At this point, Japan would still be reluctant to undertake regular patrol responsibilities away from the home islands because of the legal prohibition against the sending of Japanese forces abroad and the fear of negative reactions from regional neighbors. These concerns could be overcome if all ASEAN states requested a Japanese naval contingent attached to U.S. forces. In sum, both ASEAN and Japanese analysts can foresee conditions that would lead to a new Japanese military role in Southeast Asia, but these conditions would have to include a serious threat that could be interpreted as potentially leading to the interdiction of sea-lanes. Even under these conditions, any Japanese military role would be subordinate to and a part of Seventh Fleet operations. An independent Japanese military role in Southeast Asia remains anathema both to the ASEAN states and Japanese leaders themselves.

Concern over Long-Term Soviet-Vietnamese Plans

ASEAN's fears over long-term Soviet-Vietnamese plans center on two unsavory possibilities: control of vital sea-lanes by the USSR and Soviet backing—both political and material—for possible Vietnamese expansion beyond Indochina. Both of these raise the prospect of Soviet participation in military actions ranging from small-scale war to a major ocean confrontation with the United States. Unlike the early 1960s, however, when the Soviet Navy was described by Khrushchev as fit only for "ceremonial" activities, it has now become a broad-gauged blue-water force equipped to challenge American sea control.

In the Soviet view, the primary obstacle to Soviet ambitions in the Third World is the U.S. Navy and its main instrument, the carrier task group. Hence, the main Soviet counter is an anti–carrier task group, the crucial units of which are cruise-missile submarines supplemented by torpedo-attack submarines and surface ships for command-control, surveillance, and targeting. These are typically equipped with surface-to-surface and surface-to-air missiles. Because the Soviets have concentrated their resources on combat at sea, they lack a shipboard-air and amphibious capability to project power ashore.[28]

Interestingly, Soviet naval attention to Southeast Asia was minimal until 1979. Throughout the second Indochina war, the Soviet Pacific Fleet did not once send a contingent for a port visit.[29] Although this may have reflected the USSR's northeast Asian orientation and the Pacific Fleet's limited capabilities through the mid-1970s, by 1980 the situation had changed markedly. Soviet military ships began to call regularly at Vietnamese ports as they transited between Vladivostok and the Indian Ocean.

The Western and Japanese awakening to the Russians' Pacific capability began with the Soviets' 1975 Okean-II exercises, involving 220 ships and encompassing all the oceans surrounding the Eurasian landmass. Demonstrating the arrival of the USSR as a major sea power, these maneuvers exhibited the Soviet ability to engage in sophisticated command and control procedures on a global basis. Japan was particularly concerned about Okean-II, for Soviet ships were deployed on all the major maritime routes to the home islands—the Sea of Okhotsk, the Sea of Japan, and two locations south and southeast of the Ryukyus—illustrating Russia's ability to cut off supplies in the event of war.

Displays of force since 1975 contrast with the caution exercised by the USSR during the American mining of the harbors and coastal waters of North Vietnam in 1972. At no time did this action raise the prospect of a Soviet-American naval confrontation. To counter a U.S. force of six carriers, 40 support ships, and over a thousand aircraft in the area, the Soviets dispatched six surface combat ships, and one diesel-powered and four nuclear-powered cruise-missile submarines. These all stayed well south and east of the Paracels.[30] The establishment of a unified Vietnam as a Soviet client state after 1978 and the consequent involvement of Vietnam on the Soviet side of the Sino-Soviet dispute, however, created new opportunities for Soviet naval deployment exactly at the time that new ships, such as a Kiev-class VSTOL (vertical short takeoff and landing) carrier, were assigned to the Pacific Fleet. The combination of enhanced naval power projection and the use of port facilities in Vietnam may permit the Pacific Fleet to break out of its northeast Asian bottleneck for the first time and challenge Seventh Fleet supremacy.

Soviet forces operating out of Camranh Bay, for example, would be on the flank of China's South Sea Fleet deployed from Whampoa, Chankiang, and Yulin. Russian naval units would also be a counter to U.S. bases across the South China Sea at Clark and Subic in the Philippines. (See Map 4.) Nevertheless, the Pacific Fleet's capabilities still re-

TABLE 18

Soviet Pacific Fleet Force Levels

	1968 Number (Percentage[e])	1973 Number (Percentage)	1978 Number (Percentage)
Submarines[a]	100 (27)	101 (30)	113 (32)
Major surface combat ships[b]	58 (29)	58 (27)	67 (29)
Minor surface combat ships	n.a.	135 (22)	113 (22)
Amphibious ships[c]	n.a.	18 (25)	18 (22)
Mine warfare craft	n.a.	n.a.	110 (25)
Auxiliary/support ships[d]	n.a.	n.a.	225 (29)

SOURCES: Totals reflect a reconciling of data from a wide variety of unclassified American, British, German, and Japanese sources. Totals for 1978 are almost exclusively from U.S., Defense Intelligence Agency, *Unclassified Communist Naval Orders of Battle*, DDB–1200–134–78 (Washington, D.C., 1978), pp. 1–4.
[a]Includes ballistic missile, cruise missile, and attack boats.
[b]Includes cruisers, destroyers, and frigates.
[c]Includes medium and tank-landing ships only.
[d]Includes a wide variety of ships such as intelligence collection vessels, tugs, icebreakers, repair ships, oilers, etc.
[e]Percentage figures show percentage of total Soviet naval forces.

main focused on neutralizing Seventh Fleet activity. The 37,000-ton Kiev-class carrier *Minsk*, assigned to the fleet in the summer of 1979, does not have the shore power projection of U.S. attack carriers. The aircraft on the *Minsk* consist of KA-25 antisubmarine helicopters and YAK-36 VSTOL fighter-bombers. The Soviet carrier's main mission is not long-range air strikes but protection of the surface fleet with which it is deployed.[31]

China and the ASEAN countries have evinced parallel concerns about Soviet naval forces deployed from Vietnam. Beijing foresees the possibility of a Soviet-supported Vietnamese assault on the Chinese-occupied Paracel Islands with Russian naval interdiction of Chinese resupply efforts. The ASEAN states are concerned about a Soviet blockade or seizure of the Strait of Malacca. As early as 1971, Malaysia and Indonesia declared that their twelve-mile maritime boundaries covered the passage. Hence, it was not an international waterway. Since then, however, no major maritime user (USSR, Japan, the United States) has accepted the claim. Freedom of transit is extremely important to all. For the Japanese, it is the jugular of oil and commerce. For the Soviet Union and the United States it is the main channel for movement of their fleets between the Persian Gulf–Indian Ocean and the South China Sea. There are alternative passages through the Sunda, Lombok, Ombai, and Wetar straits in Indonesia, but these would greatly increase both cost and time. (See Map 5.) While supertankers currently use the alternate straits, most Soviet and American military shipping continues to go through Malacca.

In general, close observers of Soviet naval developments in Asia

TABLE 19

Soviet Pacific Fleet Aircraft Inventory, 1978

	Number	Percentage[c]
Strike/bombers	95	23
Tactical support[a]	85	35
Antisubmarine warfare[b]	115	32
Transport and training	60	21
TOTAL	355	27

SOURCES: U.S., Defense Intelligence Agency, *Unclassified Communist Naval Orders of Battle*, DDB–1200–134–78 (Washington, D.C., 1978), p. 4. See also Robert P. Berman, *Soviet Air Power in Transition* (Washington, D.C.: Brookings Institution, 1978), p. 43.
[a]Includes reconnaissance, electronic warfare, and tanker aircraft.
[b]Includes both fixed-wing aircraft and helicopters.
[c]Percentage figures show percentage of total Soviet naval forces.

agree that by 1980 the Soviet Navy could provide sea and air lifts to clients and also constrain U.S. naval reactions to local developments unfavorable to American clients. More important, the Soviets also appeared to be acquiring the ability to "neutralize U.S. reactions from the sea against Soviet defensive interventions on land in support of defeated clients." By extension, this may also mean that the Soviets could counteract American interventions to protect its clients.[32]

By mid-1979, U.S. officials reported that Soviet personnel were involved in ferrying VPA forces to various points throughout Indochina.

MAP 4
SOVIET NAVAL BASES

SOURCE: *New York Times*, November 6, 1978.

Assistant Secretary of State Holbrooke referred to this as "a significant new development." He went on to note that Soviet military use of Camranh and Da Nang not only provided the Russians with increased reconnaissance and intelligence capability but also new bases for possible military confrontations with other forces in the region.[33] By using Da Nang, Soviet Tupolev 95-D "Bear" reconnaissance planes can double the area they had originally covered when flying out of Vladivostok. In effect, the Russians are now capable of monitoring all Chinese, Japanese, and American naval movements from the Sea of Japan through the Indian Ocean.

The Russians insist that their operations out of Da Nang and Camranh Bay simply consist of the normal intercourse between friendly states and that they seek no base rights. It is this writer's impression, however, that since mid-1979, Vietnamese media have been conspicuously quiet on the subject. Prior to that time, however, SRV officials regularly and heatedly denied the existence of any agreement to provide the Soviets with Vietnamese bases.

American concern over Russian bases increased in 1980 with the Soviet occupation of Afghanistan. Drawing closer to China's strategic view, U.S. officials also spoke of a link between developments in Southwest and Southeast Asia. Holbrooke warned:

> . . . the Soviet Union has established a foothold in Vietnam, giving Soviet forces access to naval and air facilities at a strategic point for their deployment to the Indian Ocean . . .
>
> It is no longer accurate—if it ever was—to make an artificial division between the Pacific and Indian Oceans; they form an indivisible sea

MAP 5
THE ALTERNATIVE STRAITS

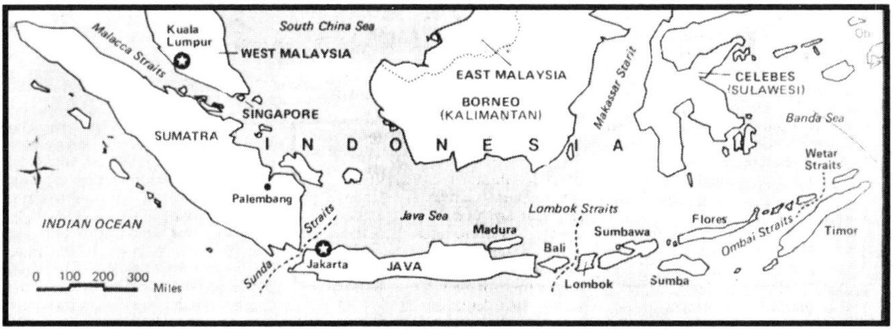

SOURCE: *Far Eastern Economic Review*, August 11, 1978, p. 66.

stretching well over half way around the globe; instability in one part of Asia can affect stability in the other. The strength of our response to Soviet aggression in southwest Asia serves our common interests with our Pacific allies and friends. And it supports and contributes to the defense of Europe as well.[34]

Holbrooke seemed to be arguing that American military assistance for ASEAN and perhaps even China would not lead to a repetition of the Vietnam war debacle. This time the goal would be to block Soviet expansion directly by countering any plans Moscow may have to link its new positions in the Persian Gulf and South China Sea, an action that could directly threaten petroleum supplies and commerce for both Europe and Japan.

Some ASEAN states (notably Singapore and Bangkok) openly condemn Soviet support for Vietnam's late June 1980 incursion into Thailand. They point specifically to the violation of Russian assurances that VPA forces would never cross into Thailand and question Russian credibility.[35] Others, such as Indonesia and perhaps Malaysia, are less testy. While politically supportive of Thailand as the front-line member, they still see the Soviet role in Vietnam as potentially useful if it is restricted to providing Hanoi a security deterrent against China. Indeed, some Indonesian analysts—in contradistinction to Holbrooke—speculate that the Russian invasion of Afghanistan could actually ease tension in Southeast Asia since the USSR may not be able to continue its heavy subsidation of Vietnam's Indochina activities.[36]

What kind of projections can be made about the prospects for war and peace (or the large grey area in between) in this new Asian cold war situation? Where might the policies discussed in this study lead?

The Future of ASEAN

Political autonomy for members of a world region as volatile and strategically located as Southeast Asia may be a pipe dream. The confluence of the Sino-Soviet and Sino-Vietnamese conflicts as well as the emergence of a Chinese-Japanese-American entente serve to embroil the ASEAN states in regional contention. Prospects for ZOPFAN recede ever further into the future as rivals for ASEAN's affections pull its members in opposing directions through a combination of promises and threats. Although the Association prefers to remain nonaligned, the powers competing for influence in Southeast Asia view its support as crucial to their regional ambitions. Nevertheless, attempts to split ASEAN's unity over regional security issues have served as an impetus

to a greater institutionalization of the Association's consultative and de-
cision-making mechanisms. ASEAN is a stronger political group in the
early 1980s because of the necessity to coalesce against competing pressures. Adversity in Southeast Asia has created a political will among the
ASEAN five to strengthen their mutual security.

As Donald Weatherbee, longtime student of Southeast Asia and political scientist at the University of South Carolina, has pointed out, neutralization as a foreign policy focus is extremely difficult to implement
because it depends not on the actions of those who desire that status but
rather on self-denying guarantees by the great powers with respect to
their own intentions.[37] International politics in the ASEAN region demonstrates that there is no such common interest in the early 1980s. Insofar as these powers give lip service to ZOPFAN, they redefine it to suit
their needs. China sees neutralization as a means of obstructing the Russian presence in Southeast Asia. The Soviets characterize the idea as a
component of their Asian collective security scheme. Hanoi opposes the
ASEAN version of neutralization, for it is essentially designed to legiti-
mize a status quo ante that would return SRV forces to their own territory and force Vietnam to dissolve the Indochina federation it forged at
so much cost.

Since Indochina cannot be integrated into ZOPFAN, the five have
reluctantly moved to a second option: encouragement of an enhanced
U.S. air and maritime presence to balance Soviet-backed Vietnamese
belligerence. Reservations over this policy exist within ASEAN, however. There is suspicion, for example, that the warmer relations between
Washington and Beijing could facilitate a larger Chinese political role
in Southeast Asia, which would only exacerbate tensions between
ASEAN and the USSR and Vietnam. This apprehension accounts for
ASEAN's lack of enthusiasm over PRC promises to come to Thailand's
aid in the event of another Vietnamese attack. By aligning with Thailand, China appears to be leading ASEAN toward a reciprocal association. Another reservation about a greater U.S. military presence is the
prospect of an arms race between ASEAN and its adversaries—a process that would deflect even more resources desperately needed for economic development.

The United States has been sympathetic to ASEAN's plight in part
because the ASEAN states are composed of political and economic systems compatible with American hopes for a liberal international order
and, more immediately, because the United States retains a strong interest in access to the region for both security and commercial reasons.
This interest implies an interest in stability. On the one hand, stability
means supporting ASEAN against external challenges from Vietnam

and, indirectly, the USSR. On the other, support for incumbent governments clashes with the American desire to see liberalization in authoritarian countries. Insofar as the United States aids friendly
authoritarian regimes to sustain their independence, it is also strengthening their ability to engage in domestic repression. It becomes virtually
impossible to separate the domestic and the international ramifications
of external aid in these cases.

Although the Soviet-Vietnamese threat to Thailand and the growing
Soviet naval strength in Southeast Asia have generated closer diplomatic cooperation on security matters among the five, the prospect of
the Association's becoming a formal military alliance remains remote for
several reasons. First, over the past several years ASEAN military forces
have received minimal budgets. Their training, tactics, and equipment
are designed to deal with domestic threats to stability and limited border
control operations. Joint maneuvers on more than a bilateral basis are
nonexistent; there have been no Association-wide military training programs or battle scenarios, nor is there a common operating language.
Moreover, the combined military strength of the five remains inferior to
that of Vietnam.

Second, differences among the five over the identity of the region's
long-term adversary inhibit any security collaboration beyond political
consultation. Malaysia and Indonesia see China as the main challenge
to the region. They are not enthusiastic about confronting or weakening
Vietnam since they view Hanoi as a buffer against Beijing. Although
opposed to Hanoi's threatening posture along the Thai border, Kuala
Lumpur and Jakarta believe that the differences between the SRV and
Thailand can be resolved through negotiations. Once these conflicts are
settled, ASEAN's cooperation with Vietnam could restore stability to
Southeast Asia. The underlying assumptions of the Indonesian and Malaysian positions are that Hanoi will rest content with control of Indochina and that the USSR is simply aiding Hanoi as a socialist ally and
has no regional ambitions of its own. At the very least these are disput-
able propositions, particularly since the kind of massive economic assistance Hanoi requires both for domestic reconstruction and to
maintain control over its Indochinese empire could be supplied over an
extended period of time only by the USSR. To argue that the SRV
would cut its ties to the USSR in exchange for ASEAN's acceptance of
a Vietnamese sphere of influence in Indochina appears unrealistic; it is
precisely Hanoi's ties to the Soviet Union that permit it to sustain this
pre-eminence.

On the other hand, assuming Hanoi has no aspirations beyond control of Indochina, ASEAN recognition of Vietnam's sphere of control in

exchange for the reduction of VPA forces in Cambodia and the loosening of military ties with the USSR could lead to a reduction in tension. If the withdrawal of most Vietnamese troops were followed by economic assistance to Hanoi from the United States, Japan, and Western Europe, the SRV could regain some of the diplomatic flexibility it lost in 1978 when it signed the Soviet-Vietnamese treaty.

Third, the Indochina situation, while the key to regional stability, is particularly intractable. ASEAN realizes that any political solution must rest on a government in Phnom Penh acceptable to the Vietnamese and Thais, and hence threatening to neither. At present, however, no contender fits these criteria. Hanoi believes time is on its side. ASEAN's resolve will weaken because of differences over China and the gradual loss of interest by the West as its attention shifts to political and economic crises elsewhere. India's recognition of Heng Samrin was particularly heartening since one nonaligned leader accepting the Vietnamese invasion of Cambodia will encourage others to follow suit.

Moreover, with massive Soviet and Vietnamese economic aid, conditions in Cambodia are improving. Rice harvests in 1980 and 1981 eliminated immediate threats of starvation and led to the termination of most emergency food assistance both in Thailand and inside Cambodia. Ironically, food supplies are actually better in Cambodia than in Vietnam because of foreign aid programs. The SRV suffered famine in 1981 as a result of bad harvests, reduced Soviet aid, a diminished agricultural labor force because of military manpower requirements, and misguided efforts to collectivize southern agriculture too rapidly. In the early 1980s, none of these problems plagued Cambodia, where Vietnamese authorities permitted private farmers unimpeded operations as a means of encouraging maximum production and differentiating Heng Samrin's leadership from that of the hated Khmer Rouge.

ASEAN insistence on indigenous arrangements for Southeast Asian security is unworkable so long as any regional actor is willing to call for outside aid, as Vietnam has with the USSR. One face-saving possibility for ASEAN could be elections designed to legitimate a somewhat more broadly based pro-Hanoi coalition government in Phnom Penh followed by the withdrawal of most Vietnamese forces from that country. But even this scenario—though favorable to the SRV—is presently unacceptable to Hanoi because it does not insure that China will abandon its provisioning of the Khmer Rouge through Thailand.

At some point, Vietnam must decide whether a reconciliation with China might not only be in its long-term political interest but also be less costly in economic terms than the current confrontation. China might be willing to accommodate a Vietnamese-dominated Indochina as long as that entity were not tied to the USSR. Hanoi could demonstrate independence from Moscow by forging new political and economic ties with the United States, Japan, ASEAN, and China itself. The restoration of Vietnam's "nonalignment" between the PRC and USSR would be a highly salutary development for regional stability: the pressure on ASEAN to devise multilateral security arrangements would diminish, and the Association would probably return exclusively to its original socioeconomic goals.

Ironically, however, the security challenges of the 1970s have provided the impetus necessary to transform a moribund economic group into the most dynamic political association in the region's history. Despite differences in perceptions of the regional threat and a lack of consensus on how to cope, ASEAN, since 1975, has created mechanisms and norms for consultation and political decisions that have been highly beneficial to the international status of all its members. The Association has helped protect a vulnerable Thailand by coalescing behind Bangkok's resistance to Vietnamese military force. ASEAN diplomacy has proven so adroit that the Western states and Japan have agreed to follow the ASEAN lead on issues of primary importance to the five. Whether this impressive performance in political and military diplomacy will affect economic interactions with developed states remains to be seen, but ASEAN in the 1980s has become a much more formidable international actor than those who observed it a decade earlier ever predicted.

Stalemate in Southeast Asia*

Often the most difficult policy for a major international actor to follow in a tense regional situation is to do nothing, especially when an existing military confrontation *appears* dangerous. Yet this may be the best advice for the United States with respect to the standoff between the Vietnam-USSR and ASEAN-China adversaries. Because of the deployment of almost 100,000 Vietnamese troops along the Thai border against the Khmer resistance operating from Thai territory (at least at times), ASEAN—by backing Thailand—has been thrust into the center of the historical Sino-Vietnamese conflict over the "permissible" strength Beijing is prepared to grant Hanoi in Indochina. For the PRC a

---

*The author wishes to express his gratitude to Professor Kernial Sandhu, director of the Institute of Southeast Asian Studies, Singapore, for his comments on these concluding remarks during an institute seminar in May 1981.

strong Vietnamese-dominated Indochina aligned with the USSR is an imminent danger to its southern border. Historically China has found analogous situations unacceptable. Similarly, for Hanoi, a Cambodia linked to an unfriendly China threatens Vietnam's independence. As long as the SRV can persuade the Soviet Union to support its dominance of Indochina, Beijing is stalemated. Moreover, *while confronting each other*, neither China nor Vietnam can threaten the rest of Southeast Asia.

Interestingly, the refugee exodus of 1979 also served to underscore ASEAN suspicions of *both* countries. On the one hand, the largely ethnic Chinese composition of the refugees from both Vietnam and Cambodia raised fears of racial imbalance and a Chinese fifth column, but on the other hand, the facts that it was Vietnam that expelled these people and Vietnam that had occupied a neighbor destroyed any sympathy the SRV had acquired in its long struggle against France and the United States.

Vietnam's diminished global prestige and China's new introspection while it concentrates on the massive task of developing its profoundly backward polity provided ASEAN not only welcome breathing space but also an enhanced international stature based on the Association's economic growth and political successes in dealing with the third Indochina war. Although Chinese and Vietnamese economic weaknesses and military vulnerabilities became apparent in their indeterminate confrontation, ASEAN, by contrast, appeared to gain political self-confidence from a series of diplomatic successes. By the early 1980s, Japan, the United States, Canada, Australia, New Zealand, the EEC, and the majority of nonaligned nations took their cues on the Indochina issue from ASEAN communiqúes.[38]

The United States centers its own regional policy on the ASEAN states, which in many ways are more stable and capable of independent action than ever before. ASEAN is partially removed from regional military tensions, which are confined primarily to the mainland among former communist associates (China, Vietnam, and the Khmer resistance). Toward these states, of course, Washington has no security obligations. The only American ally potentially involved militarily (Thailand) is located at the periphery of these conflicts. Any significant threat to its territorial integrity—barring an improbable Sino-Thai alliance to oust the Vietnamese from Cambodia—is most unlikely. The prospect of ASEAN's direct involvement in regional military action remains quite low. Hence, ASEAN can afford to berate Hanoi in international meetings, for the Association incurs virtually no political costs by doing so.

Since neither conventional military aggression nor competitive Chinese and Vietnamese aid to local insurgencies threaten the ASEAN five, the security situation on Southeast Asian land borders appears reasonably stable or at worst controllable—as in the past—through regional cooperative efforts. Washington's attentions are best directed elsewhere.

America's strategic concerns over the next several years should, therefore, center on the waters of the region—particularly the maintenance of open sea-lanes from the Persian Gulf–Indian Ocean through the China Sea. Freedom of the sea serves a number of American ends including the promotion of trade and investment with the Asian-Pacific region, which now exceed America's European commerce; the protection of Japan, which, as Washington's key Asian partner, must ply unimpeded waterways to obtain the petroleum necessary to fuel its economy; and the protection of other important Asian states, including ASEAN members, South Korea, and Taiwan.

Although it may be desirable to assist in a negotiated solution to the Indochina conflict that would eliminate the presence of Vietnamese troops on the Thai border, in all probability the status quo will persist for some time. While political costs to the United States are inherent in this situation, potential benefits also accrue. There are two major costs, one of which has already been partially discounted—the possibility of a large-scale Vietnamese thrust into Thailand, which could lead to a call for American military involvement as well as to retaliation from China. The danger in this scenario lies in the possibility of a direct confrontation among China, the Soviet Union, and the United States. Such a prospect is unlikely, however, both because all parties are aware of the inherent dangers and, more important, because Vietnam possesses neither the ambitions nor the capabilities to move beyond Indochina. Control of those three states has stretched Hanoi's military, economic, and administrative capacities severely and mortgaged its commercial future to the Soviet Union.

It is the second cost that, over time, is more worrisome. In return for underwriting the SRV's hegemony in Indochina, the Soviets have obtained excellent base facilities in Vietnam and possibly Cambodia (the port of Kompong Som). From these ports and airfields, the Soviet Pacific Fleet can bunker and provision naval and air forces, allowing them to stay on station in the Persian Gulf–Indian Ocean–South China Sea region for much longer periods. Before 1979 no Soviet aircraft operated in Southeast Asia and naval cruises had to originate from Vladivostok and Petropavlovsk. In effect, Indochinese bases have enhanced the Pacific Fleet's operational capabilities by at least one-third.

The danger from a growing Soviet Pacific Fleet operating from

Southeast Asian bases lies less in the prospect of a military showdown with the U.S. Seventh Fleet than in the political influence that attends the projection of naval force. With Russian naval and air forces regularly moving through ASEAN waters and testing their defense communications systems, an intimidating political atmosphere could develop unless countervailing American and regional forces are created. In the absence of such forces, ASEAN leaders could well conclude that accommodation of Soviet interests would be a better means of preventing Soviet interference in regional affairs than a policy of resistance or efforts to isolate the USSR would be.

The political impact of the Soviet military presence in Southeast Asia could be reduced in two ways. One, the less likely to be realized, would be the reduction of Soviet links to Vietnam following a negotiated settlement of the confrontation between Indochina and China (and ASEAN). Soviet strategic benefits from the current relationship are considerable, and the estimated financial cost to Moscow (between U.S. $1–2 billion per year) seems bearable. So long as Vietnam's border conflict with Thailand remains at a low level and China is deterred from administering a second lesson by the presence of VPA forces in depth along the Sino-Vietnamese frontier as well as by Hanoi's Soviet alliance, diplomatic efforts to convince Hanoi to reduce its ties to the Soviet Union will be ineffective. Assuming that the Soviet-Vietnamese alliance is sustained, an alternative U.S. strategy is necessary: the development of a countervailing military capacity.

Since 1980, Washington seems to have been moving gradually in this direction. By abandoning the swing strategy of sending Seventh Fleet elements to Europe in the event of a crisis there, American planners re-emphasized Asia's importance in Washington's strategic calculus. Explicit commitments to the security of Japan and Korea persist as do bilateral security ties to the Philippines and Thailand and the ANZUS treaty linking Australia, New Zealand, and the United States. In the aggregate these commitments require a capacity to maintain freedom of passage through Asian straits and waterways. Without this, ASEAN's growing intercourse could become hostage to an aggressive outside power. With Backfire-B bombers in Indochina, the Soviets have an antiship and ground attack capability of 3,500 miles—without refueling. These same Indochina bases serve as supply locations for the Soviet Pacific Fleet's Indian Ocean patrols. Based only 700 nautical miles from Subic Bay, Russian aircraft have tested Philippine airspace and fly regularly over the disputed Spratly islands, presumably on Vietnam's behalf.

Cognizant of these developments, first the Carter and then the Reagan administration pledged a gradual increase in American naval and air capabilities in the Pacific. By balancing the continued growth of the Soviet Pacific Fleet, American forces allow ASEAN and other Asian states to continue to resist involvement in the Sino-Soviet-Vietnamese imbroglio and to avoid joining either China's antihegemony front or the Soviets' Asian collective security system. In contrast, any pullback of U.S. military forces from the ASEAN area to the mid-Pacific in the Asian strategic environment of the 1980s would degrade Washington's ability to project and sustain naval and air power in the South China Sea and Indian Ocean. Any such reduction of force would reduce the United States' utility to ASEAN and would be opposed by ASEAN members so long as the Soviet-Vietnamese alliance continues and Russian ships and planes are based in Indochina.

But the United States should no longer have to defend the ocean lanes from the Sea of Japan to the Persian Gulf by itself. The *pax Americana* ended almost a decade ago. While America remains the world's pre-eminent military power, it has ceased to be the only dominant power. Its allies and other friendly states must contribute to an ability to maintain freedom of the seas against an unprecedented Soviet naval deployment in the Pacific region. A growing Japanese naval capacity based on P-3Cs and F-15s acquired during the 1980s could increasingly perform the task of monitoring the waters of the home islands and the nearby western Pacific. Australia has inaugurated Indian Ocean patrols, and Malaysia and Indonesia have begun to acquire the air and naval units needed to watch the seas around their shores as well.

Since the ASEAN states reject the prospect of Japanese ships escorting tankers to the Straits of Malacca, Lombok, and Sunda, Malaysia and Indonesia should at least develop their own abilities, in cooperation with the U.S. Seventh Fleet, to keep these waters open to international commerce. They have taken some steps in this direction. In May 1981, Jakarta opened a new airbase with A-4 bombers and OV-10 fighters on the Natuna islands.[39] Malaysia should have a new airfield and an expanded air force consisting of A-4s and F-5s ready by mid-decade. The Philippines' dispute with Vietnam over the Spratly Islands may well have given it the incentive to engage in naval surveillance. Toward this end the Philippine air force recently purchased Fokker-17 surveillance aircraft.

All of these capacities mutually reinforce America's Pacific security interests, and Washington should support these efforts by providing military credits and sales on easy terms. The 1980s portend, then, not a U.S. military withdrawal from Southeast Asia but a strategy emphasizing air and naval deployments in cooperation with friendly states to maintain the freedom of commercial routes and to deter Soviet or Vietnamese expansionism and military intervention.

Moreover, as the ASEAN states develop regional maritime defenses, their vulnerability to outside political pressures for alignment should decrease. This, in turn, would make the region a less tempting political target to the USSR and Vietnam or even to a modernized China.

NOTES

Chapter One

1. See the discussion in Earl C. Ravenal, *Strategic Disengagement and World Peace: Toward a Noninterventionist American Foreign Policy* (San Francisco: Cato Institute, 1979) pp. 10, 12, 13. This reluctance to tie U.S. fortunes to Third World development is also reflected in the decline of American security assistance by 25 percent over the past twenty years (See James Reston, "Yale Man at Harvard," *New York Times*, June 8, 1980, p. E19). The U.S. now ranks thirteenth among seventeen donor nations, with only 0.27 percent of its gross national product going for development assistance (*New York Times*, June 10, 1980).

2. Raymond Cohen, "Rules of the Game in International Politics," *International Studies Quarterly* 24, no. 1 (March 1980): 134.

3. A useful discussion appears in Murugesu Pathmanathan, *Conflict Management in Southeast Asia: A Neutralized Malaysia?* University of Malaya Occasional Paper on Malaysian Socio-Economic Affairs, no. 7 (Kuala Lumpur, n.d.), p. 13. For a more general view of the rationale for partial U.S. disengagement in Asia, see Harry G. Gelber, "America, the Global Balance, and Asia," *Asian Survey* 19, no. 12 (December 1979): 1150–1153.

4. Franklin B. Weinstein, *Indonesian Foreign Policy and the Dilemma of Dependence* (Ithaca, N.Y.: Cornell University Press, 1976), pp. 183, 184, 186, 187.

5. Guy Parker, Frank Golay, and Cynthia Enloe, *Diversity and Development in Southeast Asia: The Coming Decade* (New York: McGraw-Hill, 1977), p. 45.

6. President Carter's address to the American Society of Newspaper Editors in Washington, D.C., April 10, 1980, as published in U.S. Department of State, Bureau of Public Affairs, *Current Policy*, no. 159.

7. *Washington Post*, January 25, 1977.

8. Daniel Southerland, "Military Aid Cuts Elate Rights Forces," *Christian Science Monitor*, May 25, 1977.

9. David Andelman, "U.S. and Five Non-Red Asian Nations to Continue Talks on Key Issues," *New York Times*, June 22, 1977.

10. Richard Burt, "U.S. Defense Debate Arises on Whether Focus on Europe Neglects Other Areas," *New York Times*, March 24, 1978.

11. Stephen Barber, "Brown's Asian Assurance," *Far Eastern Economic Review*, March 3, 1978, pp. 25–26.

12. "U.S. and Philippines Reach Accord on Aid and Use of Military Bases," *New York Times*, January 1, 1979.

13. See, for example, the editorial in the *New Straits Times* (Kuala Lumpur), January 26, 1979.

14. Bernard Gwertzman, "Carter Says U.S. Warned Vietnam and Soviets Not To Threaten Thais," *New York Times*, January 18, 1979; and Henry Kamm, "Thai Premier . . . Expresses Need For Defense Aid," ibid., February 1, 1979.

15. *Nation Review* (Bangkok), June 26, 1979; and Kyodo dispatch, July 13, 1979, in Foreign Broadcast Information Service (FBIS), *Daily Report Asia/Pacific*, July 13, 1977, p. J1.

16. ANTARA dispatch (Jakarta), May 4, 1979, in FBIS, *Daily Report Asia/Pacific*, May 4, 1979, p. N1.

17. Agence France Press (AFP) dispatch (Hong Kong), May 15, 1980, in FBIS, *Daily Report Asia/Pacific*, May 16, 1980, p. P1.

18. Franklin Weinstein, "U.S.-Vietnam Relations and the Security of Southeast Asia," *Foreign Affairs* 56, no. 4 (July 1978): 848–49.

19. See the discussion in Bruce Grant, *The Security of Southeast Asia*, Adelphi Paper no. 142 (London: International Institute of Strategic Studies, 1978), p. 24.

20. See the excellent discussion in Donald E. Weatherbee, "U.S. Policy and the Two Southeast Asias," *Asian Survey* 18, no. 4 (April 1978): 412, 413.

21. Dick Wilson, "ASEAN and Indochina: Future Relations," *Asia/Pacific Community*, Summer 1978, pp. 20–23.

22. This argument is elaborated in Justus M. van der Kroef, "National Security, Defense Strategy, and Foreign Policy Perceptions in Indonesia," *Orbis* 20, no. 2 (Summer 1976): 480–81.

23. Murugesu Pathmanathan, "Conflict Management in Southeast Asia," a paper presented to the Institute of Commonwealth Studies, London, May 1974, pp. 8–9.

24. Quoted in Charles E. Morrison and Astri Suhrke, *Strategies of Survival: The Foreign Policy Dilemmas of Smaller Asian States* (St. Lucia: University of Queensland Press, 1978), p. 160.

25. Jakarta domestic service commentary in Indonesian, February 26, 1977, in FBIS, *Daily Report Asia/Pacific*, March 1, 1977, p. N1.

26. AFP dispatch (Hong Kong), July 7, 1978, in FBIS, *Daily Report Asia/ Pacific*, July 7, 1978, p. K1.

27. *People's Daily*, July 31, 1978, in FBIS, *Daily Report People's Republic of China*, August 11, 1978, p. A10.

28. See the editorials in Bangkok's *Nation Review* and *Post*, September 11 and 12, 1978.

29. Rodney Tasker, "A Courteous Rebuff for Dong's Diplomacy," *Far Eastern Economic Review*, September 29, 1978, p. 8.

30. Kuala Lumpur domestic service in English, November 13, 1978, in FBIS, *Daily Report Asia/Pacific*, November 14, 1978, p. O1.

31. Bangkok domestic service in Thai, January 22, 1979; and *Athit* (Bangkok), January 18, 1979. Both may be found in FBIS, *Daily Report Asia/ Pacific*, January 23, 1979, p. J5.

32. Kyodo dispatch (Tokyo), March 29, 1979.

33. Kuala Lumpur international service in English, April 20, 1979, in FBIS, *Daily Report Asia/Pacific*, April 17, 1979, p. O1.

34. Quoted in James P. Sterba, "ASEAN's Members Start to Speak," *New York Times*, May 4, 1979.

35. Editorial in the *Straits Times* (Singapore), May 11, 1979.

36. *Bangkok Post*, May 8, 1979.

37. For text of China's proposal at the U.N. Disarmament Commission, see Xinhua dispatch, May 16, 1979, in FBIS, *Daily Report People's Republic of China*, May 16, 1979, p. A1.

38. *Far Eastern Economic Review*, June 15, 1979, p. 15.

39. Joint communiqué of the January 5, 1980, Indochinese Foreign Ministers' Conference as carried by Vientiane domestic service in Lao, January 7, 1980, in FBIS, *Daily Report Asia/Pacific*, January 7, 1980, p. H7.

40. Author's interview, Kuala Lumpur, July 3, 1979.

41. Author's interview with U.S. embassy official, Bangkok, July 3, 1979.

42. Author's interview with U.S. embassy official, Jakarta, July 2, 1979.

43. There is a vast literature dealing with this approach to political instability. One of the classics is Ted Robert Gurr, *Why Men Rebel* (Princeton, N.J.: Princeton University Press, 1971).

44. Cited in Franklin Weinstein, "The Meaning of National Security in Southeast Asia," *Bulletin of the Atomic Scientists*, November 1978, p. 25.

45. Frank Frost, "Political Issues in Australia-ASEAN Relations, *Asia Pacific Community*, no. 7 (Winter 1980); 142–43.

46. See the discussion in Morrison and Suhrke, *Strategies of Survival*, pp. 214, 215, 217, 237.

47. Cited in L. D. Stifel, "ASEAN Cooperation and Economic Growth in Southeast Asia," *Asia Pacific Community*, no. 4 (Early Summer 1979): 134.

48. Far Eastern Economic Review, *Asia Yearbook, 1980* (Hong Kong, 1980), pp. 82–83.

49. Much of the ensuing discussion is drawn from Franklin Weinstein, "Multinational Corporations and the Third World: The Case of Japan and Southeast Asia," *International Organization* 30, no. 3 (Summer 1976): 397–99.

50. Author's interview with staff members of the Philippine Center for Advanced Studies, Manila, June 18, 1979.

51. Author's interview with ASEAN division officials of the Philippine Ministry of Foreign Affairs, Manila, June 22, 1979.

52. *New York Times*, January 9, 1978.

53. *Far Eastern Economic Review*, September 1, 1978, p. 35.

54. Much of the ensuing discussion is drawn from the excellent article by Ho Kwon Ping, "The Mortgaged New Society," *Far Eastern Economic Review*, June 29, 1979, pp. 25, 26, 51–56.

55. The World Bank report is extensively summarized in Ho Kwon Ping, "Thailand's Broken Rice Bowl," *Far Eastern Economic Review*, December 1, 1978, pp. 40–46.

56. Press Foundation of Asia, *Data Asia* (Manila), March 5–11, 1979, p. 6090, and September 24–30, 1979, p. 6542. See also *Asiaweek*, June 1, 1979, p. 34.

57. Tables 3–9 are taken from Donald Crone, "ASEAN Regionalism and the Limits of Trade Dependence," paper presented to the International Studies Association, Los Angeles, March 1980. They were computed from International Monetary Fund, *International Financial Statistics Yearbook, 1979* (Washington, D.C., 1979). The ensuing discussion is drawn from Crone's paper.

58. Tables 10–15 are taken from Donald Crone, "Emerging Trends in the Control of Foreign Investment in ASEAN," paper presented to the Canadian Political Science Association, Ottawa, May 1980.

59. In 1975, 43 percent of Singapore's exports were manufactured goods; for the other four the average was only 15 percent. See table 1 in ibid.

60. Ibid., p. 4.

61. Ibid., pp. 17–18.

62. Weinstein, "Multinational Corporations and the Third World," p. 380; and author's interviews in the ASEAN states, spring 1981.

63. Interviews with faculty of the National Defense College, Tokyo, July 1979 and May 1981.

64. Franklin Weinstein, "Multinational Corporations and the Third World," p. 396.

Chapter Two

1. A Moro official who surrendered in the Philippines in mid-1980 stated that the rebels received training in Sabah with Libyan financial assistance. President Marcos stated that discussion over this alleged assistance was continuing under ASEAN auspices. (See AFP dispatches (Hong Kong), June 8 and 10, 1980, in FBIS, *Daily Report Asia/Pacific*, June 10, 1980, pp. P1–P2.)

2. Rodney Tasker, "Slow Going on Sabah," *Far Eastern Economic Review*, May 12, 1978, pp. 28–30.

3. Statement from the Islamic Foreign Ministers' Conference in Islamabad, Kuala Lumpur domestic service, May 20, 1980, in FBIS, *Daily Report Asia/Pacific*, May 21, 1980, A13.

4. Interview with Dr. Murugesu Pathmanathan of the University of Malaya Faculty of Economics and Administration, Kuala Lumpur, July 6, 1979.

5. Peter Lyon, "The Security Policy of Indonesia: Perspectives, Functions, Prospects," paper prepared for the University of Illinois Symposium on the Security Policies of Emerging Nations, Urbana, May 15–17, 1980, p. 8.

6. See the discussion in the Press Foundation of Asia, *Data Asia* (Manila), March 17–30, 1980, p. 6938.

7. Kuala Lumpur domestic service, October 24, 1979, in FBIS, *Daily Report Asia/Pacific*, October 25, 1979, p. O1.

8. See AFP dispatches (Hong Kong), dated April 8, May 30, and June 3 1980, found respectively in FBIS, *Daily Report Asia/Pacific*, April 9, 1980, p. O1; May 30, 1980, p. P1; and June 4, 1980, p. P1.

9. For more elaboration, see Charles Morrison and Astri Suhrke, *Strategies of Survival: The Foreign Policy Dilemmas of Smaller Asian States* (St. Lucia: University of Queensland Press, 1978), pp. 163–64; and Sheldon W. Simon, "The ASEAN States: Obstacles to Security Cooperation," *Orbis*, Summer 1978, pp. 415–34.

10. Quoted in Justus M. van der Kroef, *The Lives of SEATO*, Institute of Southeast Asian Studies, Occasional Paper no. 45 (Singapore, 1976), p. 3.

11. These trial balloons are discussed in Dick Wilson, "Future Relations: ASEAN and Indochina," *Asia Pacific Community*, no. 1 (Summer 1978): 22.

12. Impediments to the formation of a military alliance are listed in Michael Leifer, "The Paradox of ASEAN: A Security Organization Without the Structure of an Alliance," *Roundtable*, July 1978, *passim*.

13. David Jenkins, "Indonesia: Taking a Defensive Position," *Far Eastern Economic Review*, July 13, 1979, pp. 15–16.

14. These figures are taken from Lyon, "Security Policy of Indonesia," p. 16. See also *Far Eastern Economic Review*, February 8, 1980, p. 70; and Barry Wain, "America and Southeast Asia: There is Hope with Reagan," *Asian Wall Street Journal*, April 22, 1981.

15. Briefing from an official with the commander-in-chief/Pacific, Honolulu, June 8, 1979.

16. U.S. Air Force briefing, Honolulu, June 8, 1979; and Joint U.S. Military Advisory Group briefing, Bangkok, June 25, 1979.

17. Interview with U.S. embassy official specializing in politico-military affairs, Bangkok, June 25, 1979.

18. Richard Nations, "Thailand Prepares to Think the Unthinkable," *Far Eastern Economic Review*, February 2, 1979, pp. 8–9; and *Asian Record*, June 1981.

19. Quoted in *Far Eastern Economic Review*, March 9, 1979, p. 17.

20. Interview with Prime Minister Kriangsak on Bangkok domestic service, August 23, 1978, in FBIS, *Daily Report Asia/Pacific*, August 24, 1978, p. J3.

21. *Far Eastern Economic Review*, June 8, 1979, p. 21.

22. These statements may be found respectively in AFP dispatch (Hong Kong), January 12, 1980, in FBIS, *Daily Report Asia/ Pacific*, January 14, 1980, p. P1; Bangkok domestic service, December 13, 1979, in FBIS, *Daily Report Asia/Pacific*, December 14, 1979, p. Jl; and AFP dispatch (Hong Kong), May 23, 1980, in FBIS, *Daily Report Asia/Pacific*, May 23, 1980, p. N1.

23. Bangkok domestic service, January 25, 1980, in FBIS, *Daily Report Asia/Pacific*, January 28, 1980, p. J7.

24. Quoted in Guy J. Parker, Frank H. Golay, and Cynthia Enloe, *Diversity and Development in Southeast Asia: The Coming Decade* (New York: McGraw-Hill, 1977), pp. 63–64.

25. See the discussion in Donald E. Weatherbee, "U.S. Policy and the two Southeast Asias," *Asian Survey* 18, no. 4 (April 1979): 410.

26. Cited in Frank Frost, "Vietnam and ASEAN: Multilateral Attitudes, Bilateral Relations and Prospects for Coexistence and Cooperation," paper presented to the Asian Studies Association of Australia (Sydney), May 14–18, 1978, p. 30.

27. Bernard Weinraub, "Vietnamese Refuse to Sell U.S. Army," *New York Times*, May 1, 1977.

28. Interview with Dr. Khein Theeravit, director, Asian Studies, Chololongkorn University, June 25, 1979, Bangkok.

29. See the article in the *New Times* (Moscow), June 3, 1977, in FBIS, *Daily Report Soviet Union*, June 14, 1977, p. B7; Radio Moscow to Indonesia, June 23, 1977, in FBIS, *Daily Report Soviet Union*, June 28, 1977; and *Red Star*, February 26, 1978, in FBIS, *Daily Report Soviet Union*, March 3, 1978.

30. The following discussion of Hanoi's decision to join the Soviet Union is drawn from two excellent reviews by the *Far Eastern Economic Review*, one in its 1979 Asia Yearbook, pp. 49–50, the other in the February 2, 1979, issue, pp. 17–20.

31. Douglas Pike, "The USSR and Vietnam: Into the Swamp," *Asian Survey* 19, no. 12 (December 1979): 1163–1166.

32. *Far Eastern Economic Review*, June 20, 1980, p. 58.

33. Drew Middleton, "NATO Fears Russia Surrounding China," *New York Times*, May 22, 1980; Press Foundation of Asia, *Data Asia* (Manila), June 25–July 1, 1979, p. 6344; *Far Eastern Economic Review*, January 4, 1980, p. 9; and *Indochina Issues*, no. 15 (April 1981): 6.

34. Conference at the Center for Strategic and International Studies, Jakarta, June 30, 1979.

35. *Pravda*, March 25, 1979, in FBIS, *Daily Report Soviet Union*, March 28, 1979, p. CC1.

36. Frederic Moritz, "Southeast Asians on a Tightrope," *Christian Science Monitor*, September 27, 1978.

37. Frederic Moritz, "Vietnam Offers Thailand an Olive Branch—and a Warning," *Christian Science Monitor*, June 3, 1980.

38. The following figures are drawn from Carlyle Thayer, "The Indochina Conflicts and Australia," paper prepared for the thirty-second annual meeting of the Association for Asian Studies, Washington, D.C., March 1980, p. 7.

39. AFP dispatch (Hong Kong), May 19, 1979, in FBIS, *Daily Report Asia/Pacific*, May 21, 1979, pp. J6–J7.

40. See Henry Kamm, "Thailand Faces Hard Choice on Cambodia," *New York Times*, December 9, 1979; and Richard Nations, "The Reality of Repatriation," *Far Eastern Economic Review*, June 28, 1979, p. 23.

41. "Thais Say Attack Drove out 100,000 Cambodians," *New York Times*, June 27, 1980.

42. Author's interviews in the ASEAN capitals, summer 1979; and *Straits Times* (Singapore) account of Foreign Minister Rajaratnam's address to the Bali ASEAN Foreign Ministers' Conference, June 29, 1979.

43. Author's interview, Kuala Lumpur, July 5, 1979.

44. Author's interview with an analyst from the Indonesian Center for Strategic and International Studies, Jakarta, July 2, 1979.

45. Cf. PRC Foreign Minister Huang Hua's address to the U.N. General Assembly, Xinhua dispatch, September 29, 1977, in FBIS, *Daily Report People's Republic of China*, September 30, 1977, pp. A6–A8.

46. Philippine Foreign Minister Carlos Romulo took this position upon learning of PRC-U.S. normalization of diplomatic relations (AFP dispatch [Hong Kong], December 16, 1978, in FBIS, *Daily Report Asia/Pacific*, December 19, 1978, p. P1.)

47. The politics of these developments and their effects on ASEAN are discussed in Sheldon W. Simon, "China, Vietnam, and ASEAN: The Politics of Polarization," *Asian Survey* 19, no. 12 (December 1979): 1171–188.

48. Chen Chu, address to the U.N. Security Council, Xinhua dispatch, January 12, 1979, in FBIS, *Daily Report People's Republic of China*, January 15, 1979, pp. A8–A10.

49. *People's Daily Observer*, June 19, 1980, in FBIS, *Daily Report People's Republic of China*, June 20, 1980, p. C2.

50. Kyodo dispatch (Tokyo), report of Mrs. Marcos's discussion with Deng Xiaoping, July 13, 1979, in FBIS, *Daily Report Asia/Pacific*, July 13, 1979, p. P1.

51. AFP dispatch (Hong Kong), March 27, 1980, in FBIS, *Daily Report Asia/Pacific*, March 27, 1980, p. O2.

52. Singapore domestic service, March 26, 1980, in FBIS, *Daily Report Asia/Pacific*, March 27, 1980, p. O3.

53. Jakarta domestic service, interview with Indonesian Foreign Minister Mochtar, May 13, 1980, in FBIS, *Daily Report Asia/Pacific*, May 13, 1980, p. N1.

54. See Peter Lyon, "ASEAN After Ten Years: Problems and Prospects for Regional and Functional Cooperation Within Southeast Asia," paper prepared for the Institute of Developing Economies, Tokyo, March 1978, pp. 14–15.

55. See the survey results taken by Franklin Weinstein, *Indonesian Foreign Policy and the Dilemma of Dependence* (Ithaca, N.Y.: Cornell University Press, 1976), pp. 145, 148.

56. *People's Daily*, January 4, 1978, in FBIS, *Daily Report People's Republic of China*, January 4, 1978, pp. E7–E8.

57. Xinhua dispatch, December 24, 1978, in FBIS, *Daily Report People's Republic of China*, December 27, 1978, p. A17.

58. Bangkok domestic service, in FBIS, *Daily Report Asia/Pacific*, January 19, 1979.

59. Suharto interview in the *Asian Wall Street Journal*, February 21, 1979.

60. *Nhan Dan* editorial, March 27, 1979, in FBIS, *Daily Report Asia/Pacific*, March 27, 1979, p. K1.

61. Xinhua dispatch, May 1, 1979, in FBIS, *Daily Report People's Republic of China*, May 2, 1979, p. E3.

62. Xinhua dispatch, May 3, 1979, in FBIS, *Daily Report People's Republic of China*, May 4, 1979, pp. E8–E9.

63. PRC Vice-Premier Chen Muhua quoted in *Bangkok Post*, June 4, 1979.

64. *Nation Review* (Bangkok), June 26, 1979.

65. Voice of the People of Thailand (clandestine CPT radio), July 10, 1979, in FBIS, *Daily Report Asia/Pacific*, July 11, 1979, p. J9.

66. Author's interviews in Bangkok with U.S. embassy officials and Thai analysts, June 24–25, 1979.

67. Hanoi international service, December 22, 1979, in FBIS, *Daily Report Asia/Pacific*, December 26, 1979, p. K4.

68. See the statement by Politburo member Le Duc Tho, Vietnamese News Agency (VNA) dispatch, December 27, 1979, in FBIS, *Daily Report Asia/Pacific*, December 28, 1979, p. K2.

69. Nguyen Co Thach interview in *Christian Science Monitor,* June 3, 1980.

70. *Pravda* interview, June 11, 1980, in FBIS, *Daily Report Soviet Union,* June 18, 1980, p. E5.

71. Quoted in the *Nation Review* (Bangkok), June 12, 1980.

72. AFP dispatch (Hong Kong), June 21, 1980, in FBIS, *Daily Report Asia/Pacific,* June 23, 1980, p. N1.

73. Singapore domestic service, March 17, 1980, in FBIS, *Daily Report Asia/Pacific,* March 17, 1980, p. O7; and *Far Eastern Economic Review,* December 21, 1979, p. 8.

74. Nayan Chanda, "Thailand: A Bid to Hold the Middle Ground," *Far Eastern Economic Review,* March 7, 1980, p. 27.

75. This analysis is drawn from interviews with Vietnamese officials by Gareth Porter, "Vietnam in Kampuchea: Arms and Options," *Indochina Issues,* no. 16 (May 1981): 1–4.

76. See the discussion in *Far Eastern Economic Review,* September 21, 1979, p. 14. See also VNA dispatch, September 8, 1979, in FBIS, *Daily Report Asia/Pacific,* September 10, 1979, pp. K1–K2.

77. AFP dispatch (Hong Kong), April 9, 1980, in FBIS, *Daily Report Asia/Pacific,* April 9, 1980, p. K9.

78. *Bangkok Post,* June 12, 1981.

79. Martin Stuart-Fox, "Factors Influencing Relations Between the Communist Parties of Thailand and Laos," *Asian Survey* 19, no. 4 (April 1979): 333–54.

80. Quoted in Press Foundation of Asia, *Data Asia* (Manila), January 8–14, 1979, p. 5761.

81. The messages are reproduced in *People's Daily,* October 2, 1979, in FBIS, *Daily Report People's Republic of China,* October 19, 1979, pp. E7–E11.

82. *Bangkok Post,* October 17, 1979. See also John McBeth, "The Ideological Crossroad," *Far Eastern Economic Review,* February 8, 1980, pp. 32–33.

83. *Bangkok Post,* November 5, 1979.

84. *Quan Doi Nhan Dan,* October 17, 1979, in FBIS, *Daily Report Asia/Pacific,* November 9, 1979, p. K17.

85. Richard Nations, "Battle for Hearts and Stomachs," *Far Eastern Economic Review,* December 7, 1979, pp. 14, 16, 21.

86. Nayan Chanda, "Hanoi Ponders the Strategy," *Far Eastern Economic Review,* December 7, 1979, p. 21.

87. Radio Beijing, in Cambodian, December 18, 1979, in FBIS, *Daily Report People's Republic of China,* December 19, 1979.

88. *Far Eastern Economic Review,* April 4, 1980, p. 7; and *Chung Pao*

(Hong Kong), March 10, 1980, in FBIS, *Daily Report People's Republic of China*, March 18, 1980, p. U7.

89. Remarks by Ladd Thomas at the Midwestern Conference on Asian Affairs, Northern Illinois University, DeKalb, October 14, 1977.

90. Hugh Peyman, "PULO Looks Abroad," *Far Eastern Economic Review*, April 17, 1981, p. 22; and K. Das, "Strife Among the Rebels," ibid., May 1, 1981, pp. 13–14.

91. AFP dispatch (Hong Kong), November 14, 1978, in FBIS, *Daily Report Asia/Pacific*, November 14, 1978, p. N1.

92. Author's interview with U.S. embassy officials, Manila, June 18, 1979.

93. A discussion of these disparities may be found in Lawrence Stifel, "ASEAN Cooperation and Economic Growth in Southeast Asia," *Asia/Pacific Community*, no. 4 (Spring/Early Summer 1979), especially pp. 143–46.

94. Pauker, Golay, and Enloe, *Diversity and Development*, p. 152.

95. Bruce Grant, *The Security of Southeast Asia*, Adelphi Paper no. 142 (London: International Institute of Strategic Studies, 1978), pp. 6–7.

96. Data for this section are drawn from John McBeth, "Separatism Is the Goal and Religion the Weapon," *Far Eastern Economic Review*, June 20, 1980, pp. 18–21.

97. Author interviews with U.S. embassy officials in Bangkok, June 24, 1979.

98. Author's interview with U.S. embassy specialist on the Thai insurgencies, Bangkok, June 25, 1979. And John McBeth, "Thailand: Communists at the Crossroads," *Far Eastern Economic Review*, July 27, 1979, p. 31.

99. *Far Eastern Economic Review*, June 16, 1978, p. 22.

100. Gordon Redding, quoted in the *Far Eastern Economic Review*, February 8, 1980, p. 82.

101. Author's interview with U.S. embassy officials, Manila, June 18, 1979.

102. The information in this section is based on an interview with a Philippine military officer in Cebu.

103. AFP dispatch (Hong Kong), May 17, 1978, in FBIS, *Daily Report Asia/Pacific*, May 18, 1978, p. P1.

104. For an analysis of the PRC-PKI relationship, see Sheldon W. Simon, *The Broken Triangle: Peking, Djakarta, and the PKI* (Baltimore, Md.: Johns Hopkins University Press, 1969).

105. David Jenkins, "The Jakarta Solution," *Far Eastern Economic Review*, September 21, 1979, pp. 38–42.

106. The percentages are for 1978, as are other figures mentioned in this section. See David Jenkins, "Giving Credit Where It Is Due," *Far Eastern Economic Review*, September 21, 1979, pp. 113–16.

Chapter Three

1. U.S. State Department briefing, Washington, D.C., May 31, 1979.

2. Quoted in Bruce Grant, *The Security of Southeast Asia*, Adelphi Paper no. 142 (London: International Institute of Strategic Studies, 1978), p. 32.

3. Ibid.

4. Quoted in David A. Andelman, "U.S. and 5 Non-Red Nations To Continue Talks on Key Issues," *New York Times*, June 22, 1977.

5. K. Das, "Double-Barrelled Border Attack," *Far Eastern Economic Review*, March 31, 1978, pp. 18–19.

6. See the editorial in Bangkok's *Nation Review*, April 27, 1978, in FBIS, *Daily Report Asia/Pacific*, April 27, 1978, p. J3.

7. These Soviet views are discussed in the *Far Eastern Economic Review*, August 26, 1977, p. 41.

8. K. Das, "Malaysia: Starting the Decade with a Bang," *Far Eastern Economic Review*, January 18, 1980, p. 30.

9. AFP dispatch (Hong Kong), May 13, 1980, in FBIS, *Daily Report Asia/Pacific*, May 14, 1980, p. O2.

10. Much of this section is drawn from John McBeth and K. Das, "A Frontier of Fear and Factions," *Far Eastern Economic Review*, June 20, 1980, pp. 16–22.

11. See note 9.

12. See McBeth and Das, "Frontier of Fear and Factions," p. 18.

13. Ibid., p. 19.

14. Hugh Peyman, "PULO Looks Abroad," *Far Eastern Economic Review*, April 17, 1981, p. 22.

15. Author's interview with Mr. C. C. Too, psychological warfare operations officer, Kuala Lumpur, July 5, 1979.

16. Bangkok domestic service, September 24, 1978, in FBIS, *Daily Report Asia/Pacific*, September 25, 1978, pp. J3–J4.

17. The communiqués were reviewed in an AFP dispatch (Hong Kong), October 16, 1978, in FBIS, *Daily Report Asia/Pacific*, October 17, 1978, p. K11.

18. *Nation Review* (Bangkok), February 7, 1979.

19. This option is discussed in a *Nation Review* editorial, March 2, 1979.

20. *Far Eastern Economic Review*, June 22, 1979, p. 18.

21. Ibid., July 13, 1979, p. 11.

22. VNA dispatch (Hanoi), October 11, 1979, in FBIS, *Daily Report Asia/Pacific*, October 12, 1979, p. K1.

23. *Nhan Dan*, November 1, 1979, in FBIS, *Daily Report Asia/Pacific*, November 1, 1979, p. K1.

24. Quoted in the *Far Eastern Economic Review*, November 23, 1979, p. 14.

25. *L'Humanité* (Paris), January 10, 1980.

26. Beijing domestic service, July 11, 1980, in FBIS, *Daily Report People's Republic of China*, July 14, 1980, p. C2.

27. Democratic Kampuchea Government statement, carried by the Voice of Democratic Kampuchea, February 15, 1980, in FBIS, *Daily Report Asia/Pacific*, February 20, 1980, p. H10; and Khieu Samphan's statement broadcast on the same radio station, March 9, 1980, in ibid., March 10, 1980, p. H8.

28. Hanoi international service, February 19, 1980, in FBIS, *Daily Report Asia/Pacific*, February 20, 1980, p. K1.

29. *Nation Review* (Bangkok), March 30, 1980.

30. K. Das, "The Kuantan Principle," *Far Eastern Economic Review*, April 4, 1980, p. 12.

31. *Nation Review* interview, May 1, 1980.

32. Huang Hua's press conference in Bangkok, AFP dispatch (Hong Kong), May 9, 1980, in FBIS, *Daily Report Asia/Pacific*, May 12, 1980, p. J2.

33. SRV Foreign Minister Nguyen Co Thach's press conference in Malaysia, AFP dispatch (Hong Kong), May 10, 1980, in FBIS, *Daily Report Asia/Pacific*, May 12, 1980, p. O3.

34. *Nation Review* on Thach's press conference, May 11, 1980.

35. Prime Minister Hussein's press conference, AFP dispatch (Hong Kong), May 13, 1980, in FBIS, *Daily Report Asia/Pacific*, May 14, 1980, p. O4.

36. Frederic Moritz, "Thailand, Malaysia Split Over How to Deal with Viet Role in Cambodia," *Christian Science Monitor*, May 16, 1980.

37. *Matichon* (Bangkok) editorial, May 21, 1980, in FBIS, *Daily Report Asia/Pacific*, May 21, 1980, p. J3.

38. Thach's press interview in Bangkok, AFP dispatch (Hong Kong), May 21, 1980, in FBIS, *Daily Report Asia/Pacific*, May 22, 1980, p. J2.

39. Nayan Chanda, "Hanoi's Signal Invitation," *Far Eastern Economic Review*, May 23, 1980, pp. 16–17.

40. ASEAN foreign ministers' statement, Bangkok domestic service, June 26, 1980, in FBIS, *Daily Report Asia/Pacific*, June 26, 1980, p. A2.

41. See the discussion of differences among the ASEAN foreign ministers in Kuala Lumpur, AFP dispatch (Hong Kong), June 29, 1980, in FBIS, *Daily Report Asia/Pacific*, June 30, 1980, pp. A5–A6.

42. AFP dispatch (Hong Kong), June 30, 1980, in FBIS, *Daily Report Asia/Pacific*, July 1, 1980, p. N1.

43. *Nhan Dan*, June 30, 1980, in FBIS, *Daily Report Asia/Pacific*, July 3, 1980, p. K5.

44. Singapore domestic service, July 3, 1980, in FBIS, *Daily Report Asia/ Pacific*, July 11, 1980, p. O3.

45. Author's interview with U.S. embassy officials, Manila, June 18, 1979.

46. Author's interview with U.S. embassy officials, Bangkok, June 10, 1981.

47. See Murray Heibert, "The Food Weapon: Can Vietnam Be Broken?" *Indochina Issues*, no. 15 (April 1981).

48. A good summary of these differences may be found in Nayan Chanda, "Cambodia: Agreement to Disagree," *Far Eastern Economic Review*, July 24, 1981, pp. 13–15.

49. Cited in Dick Wilson, "Future Relations: ASEAN and Indochina," *Asia/Pacific Community*, Summer 1978, pp. 22–23.

50. For a brief discussion of the current Indochina conflict set in historical perspective, see Sheldon W. Simon, "New Conflict in Indochina," *Problems of Communism*, Summer 1978, pp. 18–38.

51. See the discussion in Selig Harrison, *The Widening Gulf: Asian Nationalism and American Policy* (New York: Free Press, 1978) pp. 192, 193, 196.

52. Richard Nations, "Thailand Braves the Border Minefield," *Far Eastern Economic Review*, February 10, 1978, pp. 10–11.

53. Jack Anderson, "Misery and Torment for the Cambodians," *Washington Post*, August 18, 1978.

54. Nhan Dan commentator, January 17, 1979, in FBIS, *Daily Report Asia/ Pacific*, January 17, 1979, p. K1.

55. Hanoi domestic service, May 3, 1979, in FBIS, *Daily Report Asia/Pacific*, May 4, 1979, p. K12.

56. Richard Nations, "The Fight to Remain Neutral," *Far Eastern Economic Review*, May 11, 1979, pp. 8–9.

57. Bernema Press Agency dispatch (Kuala Lumpur), November 10, 1979, in FBIS, *Daily Report Asia/Pacific*, November 13, 1979, p. O1.

58. Jakarta domestic service, November 15, 1979, in FBIS, *Daily Report Asia/Pacific*, November 16, 1979, p. N2.

59. Bangkok domestic service, November 16, 1979, in FBIS, *Daily Report Asia/Pacific*, November 19, 1979, p. J1.

60. U.S. State Department briefing, Washington, D.C., May 31, 1979.

61. Author's interview with Dr. Khien Theeravit, director of Asian Studies, Chololongkorn University, Bangkok, June 25, 1979.

62. Bangkok domestic service, December 21, 1979, in FBIS, *Daily Report Asia/Pacific*, December 26, 1979, p. J6.

63. Helen Ester, "The Regeneration of Hope," *Far Eastern Economic Review*, January 4, 1980, pp. 10–11.

64. Editorial in *Indonesia Times* (Jakarta), March 24, 1980.

65. Richard Nations, "Prem Takes Peace Hopes One Step Further," *Far Eastern Economic Review*, May 9, 1980, p. 12.

66. SPK dispatch (Phnom Penh), June 8, 1980, in FBIS, *Daily Report Asia/ Pacific*, June 9, 1980, pp. H3–H4.

67. *New York Times,* June 18, 1980.

68. Associated Press dispatch, June 25, 1980; *New York Times,* June 24, 1980; and *Far Eastern Economic Review,* July 4, 1980, p. 13.

69. AFP dispatch (Hong Kong), June 25, 1980, pp. A7–A8; and *Christian Science Monitor,* June 25, 1980.

Chapter Four

1. Bruce Grant, *The Security of Southeast Asia,* Adelphi Paper no. 142 (London: International Institute of Strategic Studies, 1978), p. 15.

2. Charles E. Morrison and Astri Suhrke, *Strategies of Survival: The Foreign Policy Dilemmas of Smaller Asian States* (St. Lucia: University of Queensland Press, 1978), p. 224.

3. Ibid., pp. 251–52.

4. Ibid., pp. 253–54.

5. Author's interviews with U.S. embassy officials in Manila, April–May 1981.

6. Cited in William T. Tow, "The JANZUS Option: A Key to Asian/ Pacific Security," *Asian Survey* 18, no. 12 (December 1978): 1224.

7. Commander-in-chief/Pacific briefing, Honolulu, June 8, 1979.

8. Ibid.

9. Chee-Meow Seah, "Major Powers and the Search for a New Equilibrium in Southeast Asia," *Asia-Pacific Community,* no. 7 (Winter 1980): 89.

10. AFP dispatch (Hong Kong), February 9, 1979, in FBIS, *Daily Report Asia/Pacific,* February 12, 1979, p. P1.

11. Quoted in *New Straits Times* (Kuala Lumpur), July 3, 1979.

12. Interview in *Far Eastern Economic Review,* November 16, 1979, pp. 14–15.

13. Xinhua dispatch, January 9, 1980, in FBIS, *Daily Report People's Republic of China,* January 10, 1980, p. B3.

14. *New York Times,* January 17, 1980.

15. See the analysis of the communiqué in *Far Eastern Economic Review,* January 18, 1980.

16. Editorial in *Indonesia Times,* March 4, 1980.

17. See Holbrooke's April 2, 1980, address to the Council on Foreign Relations, New York City. It is unclear, however, whether the Reagan administration offers the same terms.

18. Quoted in John Edwards, "Washington's Pacific Thrust," *Far Eastern Economic Review,* June 13, 1980, pp. 36, 39, 40.

19. Richard Burt, "White House Expands U.S. Role in Southeast Asia," *New York Times*, July 10, 1980; and John Cooley, "Arms Aid to Thailand: Too Little, But Maybe Not Too Late," *Christian Science Monitor*, July 3, 1980.

20. Richard Halloran, "U.S. Sends New Force of Marines to Indian Ocean," *New York Times*, July 17, 1980.

21. See the discussion in Donald Hellmann, "Japan and Southeast Asia: Continuity Amidst Change," *Asian Survey* 19, no. 12 (December 1979): 1190–193.

22. See, for example, the discussion in Teik-Soon Lau, "Uncertain Prospects for Japan-ASEAN Relations," *Asia-Pacific Community*, no. 4 (Spring/Early Summer 1979): 9–20.

23. Kyodo dispatch (Tokyo), February 5, 1979, in FBIS, *Daily Report Asia/Pacific*, February 5, 1979, p. C6.

24. Henry Scott-Stokes, "Japan Asks Caution on Indochina Issue," *New York Times*, February 25, 1979.

25. Kyodo dispatch (Tokyo), April 29, 1980, in FBIS, *Daily Report Asia/Pacific*, May 1, 1980, p. C5.

26. Author's interview at the Philippine Ministry of Foreign Affairs, June 22, 1979.

27. Author's interview with Professor Isao Iwashima, Japan National Defense College, Tokyo, July 11, 1979.

28. James M. McConnell, "Doctrine and Capabilities," in Bradford Dismukes and James McConnell, eds., *Soviet Naval Diplomacy* (New York: Pergamon Press, 1979), pp. 12, 13, 22, 23.

29. Charles C. Petersen, "Showing the Flag," in Dismukes and McConnell, *Soviet Naval Diplomacy*, p. 91.

30. See the discussion in Abram M. Shulsky, "Coercive Diplomacy," in Dismukes and McConnell, *Soviet Naval Diplomacy*, pp. 134–35.

31. See the discussion in Drew Middleton, "Soviet Extends Power of Navy to all Oceans," *New York Times*, March 26, 1979. See also A. W. Grazebrock, "The Significance of the *Ivan Rogoff*," *Pacific Defense Reporter*, May 1979, pp. 7–8; and McConnell and Dismukes, *Soviet Naval Diplomacy*, pp. 281–316.

32. McConnell and Dismukes, *Soviet Naval Diplomacy*, pp. 308–9.

33. Statement by Assistant Secretary of State Richard Holbrooke to the House Foreign Affairs Subcommittee on Asian and Pacific Affairs, June 13, 1979, as released by the U.S. International Communications Agency, Kuala Lumpur (KL/6/79/65), June 25, 1979, p. 7.

34. Address by Assistant Secretary of State Richard Holbrooke to the Women's National Democratic Club, Washington, D.C., March 27, 1980, in U.S. Department of State, Bureau of Public Affairs, "U.S. Position in the Pacific in 1980," *Current Policy*, no. 154, p. 4. For a comparable high-level PRC view,

see the interview with Deputy Prime Minister Li Xiannian by Harrison Salisbury in the New York Times, July 27, 1980.

35. Singapore Foreign Ministry statement reported by Singapore domestic service, July 3, 1980, in FBIS, Daily Report Asia/Pacific, July 8, 1980, p. O1.

36. Far Eastern Economic Review, May 9, 1980, p. 13.

37. Donald E. Weatherbee, "U.S. Policy and the Two Southeast Asias," Asian Survey 18, no. 4 (April 1978): 412.

38. See the insightful discussions of Roger Kershaw, "Multipolarity and Cambodia's Crisis of Survival," and Huynh Kim Kanh, "Vietnam: Into the Third Indochina War," in Southeast Asian Affairs, 1980 (Singapore: Institute for Southeast Asian Studies, 1980), pp. 161–190, 327–346.

39. Straits Times (Singapore), May 19, 1981.

INDEX

Afghanistan, 60, 61, 97, 116–19 passim, 129, 130
ANZUS, 137
"Archipelago principle," 40
Asian Development Bank, 25
Association of Southeast Asian Nations (ASEAN), 1, 2, 3, 5; outside guarantees, 2, 5, 8, 9, 12, 18, 60, 61, 112, 118, 120, 131, 137, 138; diplomatic coordination, 3, 4, 10, 15–18, 38, 48, 61, 93–102 passim, 107, 109, 112, 131–34 passim; and Vietnam, 3, 10, 14–18 passim, 48, 49, 53, 58, 59, 62–71 passim, 74, 75, 76, 92–110 passim, 118, 131–38 passim; and Cambodia, 3, 62, 68, 69, 94–99 passim, 133; and China, 9, 15–18 passim, 49, 58–70 passim, 75, 88, 94, 103, 104, 110, 131–34 passim; security considerations, 11–18 passim, 38–111, 112, 123, 124, 131–39 passim; Declaration of ASEAN Concord and Treaty of Amity (1976), 11, 12, 20, 38, 43, 87; economic policies, 20–32 passim,

Association of Southeast Asian Nations (ASEAN) (continued) 36, 79, 80, 83, 112, 121–24; Kuala Lumpur Summit (1977), 38
Australia, 2, 9, 13, 40, 95, 135, 137, 138

Bali Foreign Ministers' Conference (1979), 95, 107, 117
Betong, 77, 78, 83, 91
Brown, Harold, 7, 115, 118
Burma, 10, 40
Bush, George, 3

Cambodia, 8, 40, 49; occupation by Vietnam, 6, 7, 12, 16, 17, 18, 50–55 passim, 60–70 passim, 75, 87, 89, 93–101 passim, 106, 109, 110, 112, 116, 119, 123, 133, 134; resistance, 47, 55, 62, 66, 98, 102–9 passim, 134; neutralization, 96–103 passim
Camranh Bay, 118, 126, 129
Cardamon Mountains, 106